Emotional and Behavioural Difficulties: Successful Practice

Edited by
John Visser

A QEd Publication

Published in 2002

© Individual chapters, their authors: Paul Cooper, Gary Hartley-Trigg, Emil Jackson, Robin Luth, Jane McSherry, Lindsay Steel.

ISBN 1 898873 26 7

All rights reserved. No part of this publication may be reproduced, stored in a retrieval system, or transmitted in any form or by any means, electronic, mechanical, photocopying, recording or otherwise, without the prior written permission of the publisher.

The right of the authors to be identified as Authors of this work has been asserted by them in accordance with the Copyright, Designs and Patents Act 1988.

British Library Cataloguing
A catalogue record for this book is available from the British Library.

Published by QEd, The ROM Building, Eastern Avenue,
Lichfield, Staffs. WS13 6RN
Web site: www.qed.uk.com
Email: orders@qed.uk.com

Printed in the United Kingdom by Stowes (Stoke-on-Trent).

Contents

List of contributors   4

Foreword   5

1 **The Effectiveness of Nurture Groups Preliminary research findings**   9
   Paul Cooper, Ray Arnold and Eve Boyd

2 **Staff Support – Lessons from experience**   18
   Lindsay Steel

3 **Including pupils with emotional and behavioural difficulties**   33
   Jane McSherry

4 **Supporting Staff – Supporting Pupils Promoting inclusion through a work discussion group offered to staff within a mainstream secondary school**   48
   Emil Jackson

5 **The electronic mirror and emotional growth: Influencing self-appraisals and motivational affects in students with EBD through the use of computer-mediated education**   62
   Robin Luth

6 **Working with CAMHS: A partnership model in practice**   75
   Gary Hartley-Trigg

Contributors

Paul Cooper is at the University of Leicester together with Ray Arnold and Eve Boyd. They have researched into the increased use of Nurture Groups in a number of settings across the UK. Paul is well known for his work in emotional and behavioural difficulties (EBD) and is currently the Editor of *Emotional and Behavioural Difficulties*.

Gary Hartley-Trigg has taught in maintained and independent sectors, all key stages, single-sex and co-educational settings and within selective and comprehensive systems. His special educational needs (SEN) experience, particularly EBD, includes residential schools, pupil referral units (PRUs) and schools for Complex Learning Needs. In the past four years he has been undertaking clinical training as an educational therapist and has trained in Solution Focused Brief Therapy. He has just started working independently as an emotional, behavioural and therapeutic consultant.

Emil Jackson is a Child and Adolescent Psychotherapist. He trained at the Tavistock Centre, London and now works at the Brent Adolescent Centre and the Tavistock Centre.

Robin Luth is special educational needs co-ordinator (SENCO) at William Ellis School in Camden. He has previously worked in day special schools, part of the local education authority's (LEA's) unified support service and as a SEN Education Officer for the City of Westminster.

Jane McSherry is an educational consultant working with individual schools and LEAs on inclusion policy and practice. She has extensive experience of working with pupils with emotional and behavioural difficulties in various settings including special schools, mainstream schools, and joint education and social service provision. She has also worked as a lecturer in developmental psychology.

Lindsay Steel runs YSP Ltd., which provides training, supervision and counselling in the educational sector. At the request of the Association of Workers for Children with Emotional and Behavioural Difficulties (AWCEBD) South East Region, Lindsay devised the Certificate in Theory and Counselling Skills in Educational Settings which has been running successfully for the past eight years.

Foreword

The Association of Workers for Children with Emotional and Behavioural Difficulties (AWCEBD) has a long and distinguished history of providing conferences and courses. These have always been well attended and appreciated by the wide range of professionals who work with pupils with EBD. They have benefited from the mixture of workshops, seminars and keynote papers that are the hallmark of the conferences. The emphasis has always been on the dissemination of good practice in meeting the needs of pupils whose special educational needs (SEN) lie in the broad continuum known as emotional and behavioural difficulties.

Professional practice does not stand still – it constantly seeks to develop. Good professional practice does this on the basis of reflection that includes examination of what was done, what outcomes were achieved and how these might inform future practice. Into this process goes the professional's past experiences, his or her discussions with others, perhaps ideas gained from attendance on a course and, hopefully, wider reading. This collection of chapters is aimed at aiding professionals in their development of good practice.

This volume is based upon presentations given at one of the AWCEBD conferences which in recent times have come to be held at the Royal College of Agriculture, Cirencester, UK. They cover a wide range of interventions from early years to adolescence, from mainstream to specialist settings. Some of the contributions report ongoing work and interventions, which are developing in a variety of settings.

Nurture Groups have become widespread following the development of Marjorie Boxall's work (Bennathan and Boxall, 1996). Paul Cooper and his colleagues, in reporting an interim stage in their study of Nurture Groups, point to the positive effects of this approach as reported by parents, pupils and schools. It is an intervention that is rooted in the developmental needs of pupils – in particular social, emotional and cognition areas. It is also an approach that builds upon a commitment to involve pupils in the identification and assessment of their SEN and engages them in the subsequent intervention. Equally, parents are encouraged to be active partners. In both these regards it accords well with government directives on partnership and voice (DfES, 2002). The emergence of this approach resonates with the resurgence of interest in psychodynamic approaches as outlined in Greenhalgh (1994) and in the practitioners' guide produced by Sharp (2001).

Jackson's contribution continues this psychodynamic theme with his emphasis upon the importance of the relationships between teacher and pupils. This chapter shows the importance of relationships in enabling the teacher to get 'behind' the behaviours of pupils with EBD and to gain an empathic understanding of the pupils' perspective. This does not excuse the child (see Visser 2000; 2002), rather it provides adults with ways of explaining to the child why the behaviour may be occurring and thus also provides him or her with alternative less damaging and more socially acceptable ways of handling their own emotions.

This has links to McSherry's contribution, which describes a structured approach to planning for the transfer of pupils from specialist to mainstream settings. Cole, Visser and Upton (1998) indicate that few pupils manage this transfer successfully, with up to two out of three pupils returning to specialist settings with all the further damage to self-worth and academic progression that this 'failing' experience entails. McSherry's chapter shows the value of carefully structuring the planning of these transitions to achieve greater success; using group work to facilitate the explorations of the emotional and cognitive demands they face in going back into mainstream education. She also points to the need to involve pupils in the identification of potential stumbling blocks and how they might be overcome.

Much has been written regarding the need to have a multi-agency approach if the systemic needs of pupils with EBD are to be met. In particular, the need for effective collaborative work in the area of health has been shown by the Health Advisory Service (1995); Cole, Sellman, Daniels and Visser (2001); and Daniels, Visser, Cole, de Reybekill, Harris and Cumella (1999). This work points to the shortcomings in provision and resources in relation to child and adolescent mental health services (CAMHS). Recent UK government publications have called for more 'joined-up' working (DfEE 1997; 1998). Gary Hartley-Trigg's chapter describes one such project where joined-up work with a CAMHS team shows what can be achieved when collaborative work is resourced. The commitment of time together with a willingness to communicate in an open and transparent manner built mutual professional respect. This in turn led to a more effective use of professional resources. He also notes the importance of involving parents and ensuring their understanding of the interventions being used with their child.

One finding from Daniels, Visser, Cole and de Reybekill (1998) confirms that mainstream settings, which are effective in meeting the needs of pupils with EBD, provide good quality teaching and learning experiences. This has been seen as an important factor for some time. Indeed it was a central finding in Wilson and Evan's (1980) study of the education of disturbed pupils. Luth in this volume shows that using information technology is a valued and valuable resource in relation to conveying to pupils the high value a school places upon their academic progression and achievement. It also shows the effectiveness of bringing to bear good quality teaching skills to provide high quality learning experiences. As a close reading of his contribution shows, it is not just the provision of pleasant surroundings and physical resources (Visser, 2001) that re-engages pupils in their education.

The chapter by Steel explores an aspect of emotion: the forgotten 'E' in EBD. She focuses on staff needs and draws upon the emerging body of literature relating to emotional literacy. Working with these children and young people can raise emotional responses within the worker. These can often be negative, such as feelings of failure, anxiety, fear and inadequacy, and can be professionally debilitating for those entering the work. They can also be emotions which are not easily admitted to and discussed with colleagues in settings where expectations of competence are assumed. Steel's contribution points to the need to be aware of the range of emotional competencies and how they can be sustained, maintained and developed.

Working with pupils with emotional and behavioural difficulties can be a very professionally draining experience (Visser, 2000). Cole et al (1998) found among the characteristics of effective workers with these pupils was the ability to go the 'extra half mile' and to take the risk of trying innovative ways of teaching and working to meet their needs. The authors in this volume reflect this characteristic. They are professionals who are quietly confident and have a secure knowledge of their professional capabilities. To take 'risks' contributes further to the professional strains of working with these pupils. What is not made explicit in the chapters that follow is the extent to which the projects were 'risk taking', nor are there explicit comments on the degree to which practitioners needed to have a secure knowledge of themselves in order to have the confidence to take the risks and engage with pupils in innovative ways.

Without these colleagues' reflections, assessment and subsequent dissemination of their work (a risk in itself), the building of a body of knowledge regarding successful practice with pupils with EBD would not become available to readers. My thanks to them for their contributions.

References

Bennathan, M. & Boxall, M. (1996) *Effective Intervention in Primary Schools: Nurture Groups*. London: David Fulton Publishers.

Cole, T., Sellman, E., Daniels, H. & Visser, J. (2001) *The Mental Health Needs of Children with Emotional and Behavioural Difficulties in Special Schools and Pupil Referral Units*. School of Education, University of Birmingham. Sponsored by the Mental Health Foundation.

Cole, T., Visser, J. & Upton, G. (1998) *Effective Schooling for Pupils with Emotional and Behavioural Difficulties*. London: David Fulton Publishers.

Daniels, H., Visser, J., Cole, T., & de Reybekill, N. (1998) *Emotional and Behavioural Difficulties in Mainstream Schools*. Research Report RR90. London: Department for Education and Employment.

Daniels, H., Visser, J., Cole, T. de Reybekill, N., Harris, J. & Cumella, S. (1999) *Educational Support for Children with Mental Health Issues Including the Emotionally Vulnerable*. A Report commissioned by the Children's Joint Planning Group, Birmingham City Council.

DfEE (1997) *Excellence for All Children: Meeting Special Educational Needs*. London: Department for Education and Employment.

DfEE (1998) *Meeting Special Educational Needs: A Programme of Action*. London: Department for Education and Employment.

DfES (2002) *Special Educational Needs Code of Practice*. London: DfES Publications.

Greenhalgh, P. (1994) *Emotional Growth and Learning*. London: Routledge.

Health Advisory Service (1995) *Together We Stand – The Commissioning, Role and Management of CAMHS*. London: HMSO.

Sharp, P. (2001) *Nurturing Emotional Literacy: A Practical Guide for Teachers, Parents and Those in the Care Professions*. London: David Fulton Publishers.

Visser, J. (2000) *Managing Behaviour in Classrooms*. London: David Fulton.

Visser, J. (2001) 'Aspects of Physical Provision for pupils with emotional and behavioural difficulties' in *Support for Learning*, Vol. 16.2 pp.64–68.

Visser, J. (2002) 'Eternal verities: the strongest links' in *Emotional and Behavioural Difficulties*, Vol. 7.2.

Wilson, M. & Evans, M. (1980) *The Education of Disturbed Pupils*. Schools Council Working Paper 65, London: Methuen.

Chapter 1

The Effectiveness of Nurture Groups
Preliminary research findings

Paul Cooper, Ray Arnold and Eve Boyd

This chapter reflects the interim report of the second phase of the University of Cambridge Nurture Group Research; a two-year national study of the personal, social and educational outcomes associated with Nurture Group placement. The project was funded by the Nuffield Foundation, the DfES and the Calouste Gulbenkian Foundation.

Phase 1

The current study has developed from our first phase study of the nature and distribution of Nurture Groups in England and Wales (Cooper, Arnold and Boyd, 1999). There were two important outcomes of this research. The first was the identification of key characteristics by which a genuine Nurture Group can be defined. Central among these characteristics are the ways in which:

- the practical, day-to-day work of the Nurture Group is rooted in an understanding of the developmental needs of children, the interdependence of social, emotional and cognitive factors, and a commitment to the fostering of positive, healthy development;
- the work of the Nurture Group is fully integrated into mainstream school and LEA policies and structures, so as to avoid the 'sin bin' trap;
- children's admission to, progress in, and eventual departure from the Nurture Group are informed by the use of appropriate diagnostic and evaluative tools, such as the Boxall Profile (bennathan and Boxall, 1998).

The second important finding was that there were four basic variations of the Nurture Group theme:

- classic 'Boxall' Nurture Groups, which accord in all respects with the model established by Marjorie Boxall (Bennathan and Boxall, 2000);
- variants on the classic model, which differ in structure and/or organisational features from the Boxall groups, but which clearly adhere to the core principles of the classic approach;
- groups, that bear the name 'Nurture Group', or are claimed to be variants on the Nurture Group concept, but that do not conform to Boxall principles;

- groups that bear the name 'Nurture Group' or are claimed to be variants on the Nurture Group concept, but that contravene, undermine or distort the key defining principles of the classic Nurture Group.

The first two variants might be seen as genuine Nurture Groups. The third variant is questionable, and the fourth variant is potentially dangerous, by promoting a distorted image of what a Nurture Group is.

Phase 2 Research questions

With these issues in mind we have embarked on the second phase of the project, which focuses on the effectiveness of Nurture Group provision. The central aim of this phase is to establish the effects of Nurture Group placement on student progress. The main research questions are:

- How do different variants on the Nurture Group approach compare in terms of their effectiveness in promoting the positive social, emotional and educational development of pupils?
- What is the impact of the Nurture Group approach on the mainstream schools they serve, in terms of mainstream teachers' perceptions and practice?
- What are children's and parents' perceptions of and attitudes towards Nurture Groups?
- What if any are the perceived effects of Nurture Groups on parents' ways of relating and dealing with their children?

Research design

The study is longitudinal in design, taking place over two years beginning in 1999. During this time the progress of students attending Nurture Groups would be measured and compared with the progress of two comparison groups:

- **Comparison group 1** was a group of children matched with the Nurture Group students for age, gender, educational attainment and level of social, emotional and behavioural difficulties (SEBD) in mainstream classrooms in the Nurture Group schools.
- **Comparison group 2** was a group of children matched for age and gender with Nurture Group students but without emotional and behavioural difficulties.

Research instruments

Levels of SEBD will be assessed and monitored for all the participants using the Goodman Strengths and Difficulties Questionnaire (SDQ) (Goodman, 1999; 1997). This is a 25-item behaviour screening questionnaire which measures five sub-scales: hyperactivity, conduct problems, emotional symptoms, peer problems and prosocial behaviour. It has been found to produce results consistent with more established behaviour rating scales, such as Achenbach's Child Behaviour Checklist and Rutter's Child Behaviour Rating Scale (Goodman, 1999). It also includes an 'impact supplement' which seeks to reveal perceptions of the level of distress and social impairment associated with the symptoms revealed by the checklist (Goodman, 1999).

In addition, students attending the Nurture Groups were assessed using the Boxall Profile (Bennathan and Boxall, 1998) and completed by the teacher. This is a detailed normative, diagnostic instrument (Bennathan and Boxall, 2000; 1998), which can be used to measure a child's level of emotional and behavioural functioning, as well as highlight specific targets for intervention within a child's individual functioning. The profile is divided into two main parts, each divided into 34 statements. The first part deals with developmental factors underpinning the individual's ability to engage effectively in the learning process. Section two of the profile deals with the child's behavioural characteristics that may inhibit or interfere with the child's social and academic performance. Each of these items is broken down into a series of sub-items that take the form of descriptive statements, which the respondent is required to rate.

Parent perceptions are accessed using a semi-structured telephone interview. Student perceptions are accessed using a face-to-face informant-style interview. Students' educational progress is assessed using National Curriculum and teacher perception data (progress in English, maths and science).

Procedures

SDQ and Boxall data was gathered on all students when they entered the Nurture Group (NG). These measures were repeated during the third term of their attendance in the NG, or upon their full-time return to a mainstream class if this was sooner. Interviews were carried out over the same period. Academic progress data was gathered annually. Comparison group data was taken over the same time scale using the SDQ only.

Participating students, schools and LEAs

The interim report is based on data from:

Students

There were 342 students, of whom 216 were in Nurture Groups and 64 were matched children with SEBD in mainstream classes, while 62 were matched children without SEBD in mainstream classes. In October 1999, 84% of primary school children were aged between 4 and 7 years, and 16% were aged between 7 and 10 years.

Schools

These students were distributed between 25 state-funded schools, of which 23 were in the primary sector and two were in the secondary phase.

LEAs

The schools were distributed across eight LEAs of varying sizes, including rural, unitary and metropolitan types, drawn from geographically diverse locations throughout England, including areas of high, medium and low levels of social deprivation. Two LEAs have markedly diverse ethnic populations.

Interim findings

It should be stressed that what follows is an account of interim findings only. The longest period of time that any student has spent in a Nurture Group is one year. Earlier research indicated that the average length of stay for students in Nurture Group was one year (i.e. three terms), with a maximum length of stay being 1.3 years, that is four terms (Iszatt and Wasilewska, 1997). It should also be noted that not all the data pertinent to our research questions has yet been processed. These findings, therefore, represent a snapshot picture which may change when the full data set is examined.

Evidence of educational, social, emotional and behavioural progress

SDQ and Boxall data show consistent levels of improvement in the mean scores across all Nurture Groups (see Table 1).

At entry 92% of NG children are in the abnormal or borderline range on the SDQ, compared with 85% of matched SEBD students. By the third term this has changed to 64% for Nurture Group students compared with 75% for SEBD students. The mean differences between these scores is statistically significant.

SDQ 1	Nurture Group students	Mainstream students with EBD	Mainstream students without EBD
Normal	8%	16%	98%
Borderline	16%	13%	2%
Abnormal	76% (92%)	72% (85%)	0% (2%)
SDQ 2			
Normal	36%	25%	97%
Borderline	21%	20%	3%
Abnormal	43% (64%)	55% (75%)	(3%)

The difference between the improvement in NG and each set of mainstream scores is statistically significant (t-test p = <.000).
Table 1: SDQ scores for Nurture Group and mainstream students

Data from the Boxall Profile scores paints a positive picture also showing statistically significant improvements in mean scores on both the developmental and diagnostic strands.

Data from teacher perceptions indicate that progress is being made in students' academic progress (see Table 2). As yet we have no comparative data against which to judge these perceptions. However, it should be stressed that lack of educational progress is a key criterion for entry into a Nurture Group.

	Worse	No change	Some progress	A lot of progress	No data
English	1	15	60	20	4
Maths	1	15	60	20	4
Science	1	15	60	10	10

Educational Progress. Figures show percentage of Nurture Group pupils in each category (N=196)
Table 2: Teachers' perceptions of progress in Nurture Group pupils

These perceptions are echoed by parents (see Table 3).

Impact on mainstream schools

There is clear evidence from interviews with teachers that Nurture Groups are perceived to have a positive influence on schools as a whole. This influence is felt in terms of the following key features:

- the development of more nurturing attitudes and practices throughout the school;
- changes in the ways in which teachers think and talk about children;
- contribution of nurturing principles to whole-school policies;
- increased sense of empowerment with 'difficult' students;
- evidence of an increased awareness of developmental issues and the relationship between social-emotional factors and learning.

Parents' perceptions of Nurture Groups and their effects

Parents' perceptions of Nurture Groups varied from negative to highly positive in terms of their effects on their child's progress and development (Table 3). The majority of parents felt that placement in the group had had a positive effect on the social, emotional and behavioural development of their children. Many parents felt that this progress would not have been made in the mainstream setting. This perception was even held by some parents who reported being at first resistant to the idea of a Nurture Group placement for their child, but who changed their view on seeing positive changes in their children which they attributed to the effects of placement. A commonly cited improvement was in the child's attitude towards school and motivation to attend. In addition the children's behaviour, both at home and school, was seen to improve. Dissatisfaction was associated with a perceived lack of progress rather than deterioration in children's performance.

Progress area	Better	No change	Worse
Behaviour	51	22	5
Educational progress	60	16	3
Enjoyment of school	54	26	4
Mean totals	55	21	4

Table shows percentage of parents nominating each category (N=89)
Table 3: Parental perceptions of their child's progress

With regard to the impact of Nurture Group placement on parent-child relationships, there is clear evidence of parents feeling less anxious and more optimistic about their child's development.

Differences in the performance of types of Nurture Group

The majority (17) of the Nurture Groups in this study conform to the 'classic' model, where between 10 and 12 children attend for 4.5 days per week while remaining on the register of mainstream class where they register daily and attend for a half day per week. The groups are located on the premises of mainstream primary schools, are staffed by a teacher and a Learning Support Assistant (LSA).

Variations on this model in the current study include:
- one full-time group (i.e. students spend all of their time in the NG);
- two groups in secondary school settings;
- five groups running on a half-time basis.

At this interim stage we have observed no statistically different outcomes between these different types of groups. One LEA, which has several Nurture Groups, appears to have students in the mainstream improving at a greater rate than those in the Nurture Group. On closer inspection the extremely atypical scores of one of the schools cause this surprising result. Other groups in the same LEA are scoring at or above the mean level achieved by the day groups.

Discussion and conclusions

The following limitations to the current report must be acknowledged in any interpretation of these interim findings:
1. The study is only half complete. We intend to approximately double the number of children and groups being studied over the final year. The data sets are, therefore, too small to generalise from.
2. We have not yet recruited a sufficient number or range of different types of Nurture Groups to draw any conclusions about the relative merits of different types of Nurture Groups.
3. We cannot assume that the current rates of improvement will be sustained. The overall effects of Nurture Group provision on the current cohort of participants cannot be judged until they have completed their period of enrolment in the Nurture Groups and are returned to full-time mainstream class placements or referred elsewhere. It will be important, for example, to compare rates of progress over this period of time with our two comparison groups.
4. We have yet to collect and analyse all of the data for our second non-SEBD comparison group.

With these qualifications in mind, the interim findings show that, in these LEAs, Nurture Groups appear to have added value to the work that schools do with children with SEBD, although it should be stressed that, on the basis of these findings, placement in the mainstream is also associated with improvements in SEBD albeit of a lower magnitude than in the Nurture Groups. This finding gives rise to a number of possibilities which the extensions to our research will explore, such as:

1. The school is the key independent variable, and schools that are effective in supporting children with SEBDs can benefit from the additional support of a Nurture Group.
2. The Nurture Group is the key independent variable. Nurture Groups can influence the climate and practices of schools where they are placed and improve the quality of response to SEBDs throughout the school.
3. Nurture Groups have no sustained influence on student progress. The findings may be an artefact of the short time-span and limited scope of the data gathered and over time the differences we have observed will disappear.

It is impossible for us at this stage to choose between these possibilities. What we can say, however, is that so far we have not found anything that would challenge or undermine the growing popularity of Nurture Group provision. This popularity is based on the increasingly widely held belief that Nurture Groups can make a significant contribution to mainstream schools by helping them to expand their capacity to cater for the needs of children with social, emotional and behavioural difficulties.

References

Bennathan, M. & Boxall, M. (2000) *Effective Intervention in Primary Schools: Nurture Groups* (2nd edition). London: David Fulton Publishers.

Bennathan, M. & Boxall, M. (1998) *The Boxall Profile: Handbook for Teachers*. East Sutton: AWCEBD.

Cooper, P., Arnold, R. & Boyd, E. (1999) *The Nature and Distribution of Nurture Groups in England and Wales*. Cambridge: Cambridge University School of Education.

Goodman, R. (1997) 'The strengths and difficulties questionnaire: a research note'. *Journal of Child Psychology and Psychiatry*, 38, 581–585.

Goodman, R. (1999) 'The extended version of the strengths and difficulties questionnaire as a guide to child psychiatric cases and consequent burden'. *Journal of Child Psychology and Psychiatry*, 40, 5, 791–800.

Iszatt, J. & Wasilewska, T. (1997) 'Nurture Groups: an early intervention model enabling vulnerable children with emotional and behavioural difficulties to integrate successfully into school'. *Educational and Child Psychology*, 14, 3.

Chapter 2

Staff Support – Lessons from experience

Lindsay Steel

Research by Rutter and Smith (1995) concluded that there was unmistakable evidence of a marked increase in psychosocial disorders over the last 40 to 50 years. Factors included unemployment, poverty and income distribution, family functioning, adolescent transactions, moral concepts, values and rising expectations. School culture alone cannot change society, but it is evident that schools are receiving more students not just with impairments to their academic abilities, but also with impaired control over their emotional lives. Goleman (1995) suggests that:

> 'As children grow ever smarter in IQ their emotional intelligence is on the decline ... a massive survey of parents and teachers shows the present generation of children are growing more lonely and depressed, more angry and unruly, more nervous and prone to worry, more impulsive and aggressive.'
>
> (Goleman, 1995, p. 11)

As young people have changed, their behaviour in schools reflects what is happening in the rest of their lives, and adults are often left at a loss how to manage with the gamut of emotions that these young people cannot help engendering in us. It could be that we are attempting to solve today's problems with yesterday's solutions, and it is simply not working.

Those of us who choose to work with disturbing children enter a totally new kind of relationship. It is all too easy to absorb the distress that these young people present, leading to feelings of helplessness and powerlessness, of being overwhelmed, even angry and frustrated. It is incredibly difficult for those working with these youngsters to feel they are 'good enough'. Expectations from outside agencies place pressures on staff to achieve quantifiable results; goal posts are changed; teaching practice is under constant scrutiny and accountability. Newly qualified staff often struggle to admit their anxieties in a culture that does not recognise that the need for support goes further than staff room cynicism. These feelings are contagious and can seriously affect the working environment – negative teacher expectations and attitudes have a profound effect on students' school success.

It is taken as read that staff have adequate intellectual ability or technical knowledge to perform their jobs, but do they possess the personal qualities to manage the stress of working with disturbing youngsters? Knowledge and cognitive skills are considered to be related to IQ; however, motivation and the desire to learn are tied to emotional intelligence. Goleman (1995) considers that IQ probably accounts for as little as 20% of life success, as learning takes place across the board and in all areas of our lives.

It is important to acknowledge the systemic nature of difficulties. This chapter concentrates on one aspect of the school system – staff and how they can best be supported in the current climate.

Over the past five years I have been working with adults who deal with disturbing youngsters and during the past two years I have been responsible for much of the training, development, counselling and supervision in one school in particular. The school has been subject to particular circumstances arising from external investigations and it is this experience more than any other that has increased my conviction that a critical aspect of staff support is developing emotional intelligence in both staff and pupils. When we are unable to change external circumstances, we need to develop internal resources to deal with our feelings and this is where emotional intelligence is vital. It is impossible to separate emotions from other important activities of our lives, however:

> 'We have to negotiate our way through the 21st Century with a brain and nervous system that have not altered their response to threat since the Stone Age.'
> (Aldridge, 2000, p. 10)

Processes going on in the brain generate an entire spectrum of emotions. An emotion is a state of mind generated at an unconscious level. We cannot help our emotions, but we can learn to control them.

> 'All emotions are, in essence, impulses to act, the instant plan for handling life that evolution has instilled in us.'
> (Goleman, 1996, pp. 6–8)

The conscious realisation of our emotions gives rise to feelings and without the ability to verbalise feelings, emotions tend to be expressed through movement and action.

Cognitive neuroscience has allowed the observation of biological functioning and the changes in brain chemistry that take place as information is processed that ultimately results in feelings.

'... in a very real sense we have two minds, one that thinks and one that feels. These two fundamentally different ways of knowing interact to construct our mental life ... Ordinarily there is a balance between emotional and rational minds, with emotions feeding into and informing the operations of the rational mind and the rational mind refining and sometimes vetoing the inputs of the emotions.'

(Goleman, 1996, pp. 6–9)

At the core of our 'emotional mind' is a small limbic structure called the amygdala. All incoming data is passed through the amygdala for emotional intensity before passing to the cerebral cortex (or rational mind) for logical processing. The amygdala stores our own unique and personal emotional history (anything that has caused us passion, rage, pain or compassion) and has been pinpointed as the area where fear and anger are generated. Research by Gardner (1993) and LeDoux (1996) indicates that individuals may have a predisposition for experiencing emotions to a greater or lesser extent and that this is rooted in biology.

The left-hand side of the amygdala responds to vocal tonal qualities in the voice and the right-hand side to the 7000 plus facial expressions within the human range. It is thought that an oversensitive amygdala may lead to people being quick to take offence, while a slow reacting amygdala may give rise to people having the appearance of being cool and detached. People with damage in the amygdala have been found to experience impaired fear responses – they cannot be conditioned to feel fear and have problems recognising fear expressions in others.

The part of the emotional brain that is capable of controlling and mediating feelings is in the neocortex. Lodged just behind the forehead, this structure is used to reappraise situations and deal with them more effectively. Once an emotion is triggered, within milliseconds the neocortex analyses the situation using memories, reasoning and language to consider possible actions and choose the most appropriate alternative. The body may have responded to the amygdala, but there are links from the neocortex to the amygdala, which can override this response. Problems will occur if the feedback links from the neocortex are not strong enough.

Ideally, these two structures will be in perfect synchrony – the amygdala signalling danger, and the neocortex selecting strategic action. However, the amygdala works more quickly than the rational brain and the data leaving the amygdala sometimes carries such a potent emotional content that it overwhelms rational thought. This leads to action with no regard for consequence and triggers a range of physiological outputs such as heart rate, blood pressure – an immediate fight or flight response – what LeDoux (1996) calls the 'quick and dirty' response. Each of us must have experienced a time when asked 'Why did you do that?' we can quite truthfully answer, 'don't know'. Goleman (1995) calls this process an 'emotional hijack'.

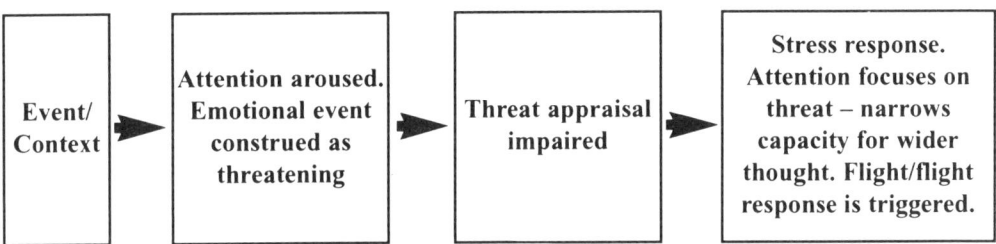

When an 'emotional hijack' occurs, the amygdala overreacts and intense emotions overwhelm reasoned thought. The neural circuits from the amygdala are creating static, sabotaging the ability of the neocortex to maintain working memory. We literally cannot think straight.

Goleman (1995) proposed that the emotional brain learns differently from the neocortex that deals with cognitive tasks. Childhood experiences and developmental levels lay down these emotional pathways, and the automatic actions they lead to. The 'emotional brain' uses 'associated logic'. It takes elements that symbolise reality, or trigger a memory of it, to be the same as reality. While the rational mind makes logical connections between cause and effect, the emotional mind connects things that have similar striking features. The amygdala scans all incoming data and when a match of any kind is made, the emotions that lie dormant are triggered. Goleman (1995) suggests that all it takes is for one element of a current situation to resemble a situation from the past for an automatic behavioural response to be triggered. The context for this emotion is stored elsewhere in the brain, so the logical brain does not recognise that some of the elements of this current situation are different. The reaction may be anything from a vague sense of disquiet to full-blown rage. This reaction is automatic, but clearly not always appropriate to the current event.

> 'The rational mind reasons with objective evidence; the emotional mind takes in beliefs to be absolutely true and discounts evidence to the contrary. That is why it is futile to reason with someone who is emotionally upset. Reasoning is out of place and carries no weight. Feelings are self-justifying.'
>
> (Goleman, 1995, p. 78)

In this way it can be understood that emotions operate 'out of time' – often an echo from the past. Only when we bring emotions to the conscious mind can we really begin to deal with them effectively – using appropriate feelings proportionate to the circumstance and conflict resolution as an alternative to a fight or flight reaction.

Physiological and personal growth come when we can face what it is that bothers us, gain an understanding of it and figure out what to do about it. However, our survival depends upon our being able to adapt to change in our environment. This means that we need to be in a permanent state of readiness or arousal. Anxiety is at the extreme end of arousal and anxiety narrows our attention. Dr Johnson famously observed, 'Depend upon it, Sir, when a man *knows* he is to be hanged in a fortnight, it concentrates his mind wonderfully.' Anxiety can cause intrusions to our functioning such as:

- waves of feeling that well up and then subside;
- preoccupation with a stressful event;
- sudden, unasked-for thoughts that have nothing to do with the mental task at hand;
- thoughts and feelings that the person cannot stop once they have started;
- excessive alertness and tense expectancy;
- insomnia and bad dreams;
- startled reactions.

When anxiety swamps attention all performance suffers.

> 'When emotions overwhelm concentration, what is being swamped is the mental capacity cognitive scientists call "working memory", the ability to hold in mind all information relevant to the task in hand.'
>
> (Goleman, 1995, pp. 78–79)

Continued anxiety causes physical and mental difficulties which eventually lead to stress. When a stress response drives attention it focuses on the threat at hand. However, stress situations in modern life rarely allow us to deal with the stress-inducing threat and dispatch it there and then. More likely we carry on with life as usual while dealing with some ongoing situation of threat: going to work through divorce, managing paying bills while coping with bereavement, etc.

Stress occurs when the demands of the environment in a person's eyes exceed his or her resources. 'In a person's eyes' is the key issue. It is not the event in and of itself (be it job loss, divorce, false allegations by a child); it depends on how the person sees the event – as a challenge ... as a relief ... as a threat? The nature and duration of the 'stressor' can lead to ill health both mental and physical. Stress is highly subjective, but if an event is perceived as an individual threat, then stress is triggered.

Aldridge (2000) suggests that the subjective nature of stress makes research into the topic difficult, but it is possible to distinguish between two main classes of stress. Firstly, trauma, such as war, physical abuse, serious road accidents, terrorist attacks and natural disasters, can overwhelm the defences of even the most phlegmatic. Secondly, there are the everyday stressors, ranging from a row with your partner to losing your parking space. There are several well-known stress rating questionnaires where the emphasis is on change, rather than the nature of stress itself. This is in line with what is known of the psychology of stress-response to change in the environment. The brain does not know if the change is positive or negative, only that something is changing.

Few of us are immune from change, pressures and stresses in our personal lives. Those working with disturbing children are also under pressure most of their working day and when events such as physical intervention, false allegations, and inspections or investigations become more common, stress would seem to be inevitable. We may be able to do little to prevent these 'stressors', but what we can do is to set up ways of managing our emotions to deal with these events with as little stress as possible. Lodge, McLaughlin and Best (1992) considered that the paucity of pastoral care for staff is a major contributory factor in stress.

Stress is the product of a cognitive act, appraisal. Many of us would recognise being subject to 'situated cognition' (Ceci and Williams, 2000) – that is a person's ability to use their cognitive processes is dependent upon a variety of 'situational variables'. Intelligent behaviour is tied to a context and once outside that context the ability is lost. For instance, we may be able to act intelligently in the supermarket queue when someone pushes in, but totally unable to manage when a youngster barges past us going through a door. This latter may be seen as a threat to our status, our self-esteem; indicate lack of respect in the young person ... yet another person pushing me about. Our sense of perspective is lost. If we can access our cognitive abilities, by avoiding an 'emotional hijack', we can then reappraise the situation:

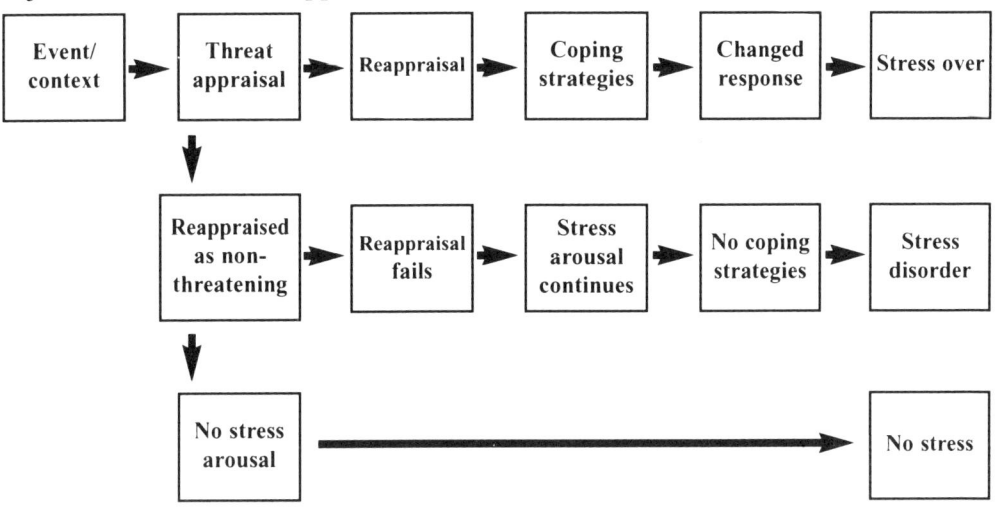

(Adapted from Aldridge, 2000)

Reappraisal may fail because of denial, which blanks the awareness of a troubling fact, perhaps because of the emotions that surround the event. Denial and intrusion both prevent cognitive processing of events. Ways of coping with a difficult event will vary according to each individual's innate orientation. 'I don't see what I don't like' or 'I don't notice what I do' may be effective temporary coping strategies, but inhibit change. Some individuals prefer to intellectualise about the event, some may need to resort to palliative ways, taking anti-depressants, for example, to enable them to respond differently to the situation. If the roots of anxiety and stress are unchangeable, that leaves room for manoeuvre only in how one perceives the problem, manages one's emotions and chooses one's behaviour.

Learning to know one's emotions and learning to manage them are the basic entry points to the development of emotional intelligence. The use of emotional intelligence can help us to make a clear evaluation of a situation, examine options and choose behaviour.

> 'Quite simply, emotional intelligence is the intelligent use of emotions – intentionally making your emotions work for you by using them to help guide your behaviour and thinking in ways that enhance your ability to satisfy your basic needs and obtain your wants.'
>
> (Bodine and Crawford, 1999, p.34)

Emotional intelligence determines our potential for learning practical skills based upon the five elements of:
- self-awareness;
- motivation;
- self-regulation or emotional management;
- empathy;
- relationship skills.

Emotional competence

If these elements can be developed, an individual will be able to utilise specific skills and abilities called 'emotional competencies'. Emotional competence demonstrates how much of this potential we have translated into our work practices. Simply being high in emotional intelligence does not guarantee the ability to display emotional competencies – but it does mean the individual has the potential to learn them. The emotional competencies can be arranged into groups based on a common emotional intelligence capacity and divided into personal and social competencies.

Personal Competencies These determine how we manage ourselves	**Social Competencies** These determine how we manage relationships
Self-awareness – knowing one's internal states, preferences, resources and intuitions. • Emotional awareness: recognising one's emotions and their effects. • Accurate self-assessment: knowing one's strengths and limits. • Self-confidence: a strong sense of one's self-worth and capabilities.	**Empathy** – awareness of others' feelings, needs and concerns. • Understanding others: sensing others' feelings and perceptions and taking an active interest in their concerns. • Developing others: sensing their developmental needs and bolstering their abilities. • Service orientation: anticipating, recognising and meeting children's needs. • Leverage diversity: respecting and relating well to people from all backgrounds. • Political awareness: understanding the ethos that shapes the climate in the organisation and the wider political agenda.
Self-regulation/Self-control – managing one's internal states, impulses and resources. Keeping disruptive emotions and impulses in check. • Trustworthiness: maintaining standards of honesty and integrity. • Conscientiousness: taking responsibility for personal performance. • Adaptability: flexibility in handling change. • Innovation: being comfortable with novel ideas, approaches and new information.	**Social skills** – adeptness at inducing desirable responses in others. • Influence: wielding effective tactics for persuasion. • Communication: listening openly and sending convincing messages. • Conflict management: negotiating and resolving disagreements. • Leadership: inspiring and guiding individuals and groups. • Change catalyst: initiating or managing change. • Building bonds: nurturing instrumental relationships with adults and children alike. • Collaboration and co-operation: working with others in the organisation towards shared goals. • Team capabilities: creating group synergy in pursuing collective goals.

Motivation – emotional tendencies that guide or facilitate reaching goals. • Achievement drive: striving to improve or meet a standard of excellence. • Commitment: aligning with goals of the group or the organisation. • Initiative: readiness to act on opportunities. • Optimism: persistence in pursuing goals despite obstacles and setbacks.	

(Adapted from Goleman, 1996)

Each of the competencies is:
- **independent** – makes a unique contribution;
- **interdependent** – draws to some extent on certain others;
- **hierarchical** – builds on each other;
- **generic** – a general list is applicable to some extent to all occupations, but the level of competency will differ according to job demands.

If we are to manage our personal and working lives in education with as little stress as possible, we need these competencies. To help to reduce stress we need the personal qualities of self-awareness, self-control and motivation. To work effectively with both staff and pupils we need the competencies of empathy, ability to listen, to influence, to collaborate and to get people motivated and working together. The management team of each school needs to consider to what extent the organisation fosters these competencies or discourages them. The degree to which the climate of the school feeds these competencies will dictate how effective and productive the organisation will be. Stress reduction and good management go hand in hand.

From experience of offering staff support and supervision in educational organisations, it seems that many staff who are suffering from stress show behaviour traits that could indicate that they are lacking in the understanding of emotional intelligence, or have fallen down in some of the major dimensions of personal and social competence. For example:

Self-awareness – unable to recognise personal strengths, they focus on weaknesses. They do not feel emotionally strong enough to reflect and learn from experiences. They are no longer open to candid feedback, new perspectives or continuous learning and seem to have lost the ability to have a sense of humour and perspective about themselves. We all have 'blind spots' and may need someone to open our eyes. Common blind spots can be: • Blind ambition – these people must be right at all costs. • Unrealistic goals – needing to appear perfect they constantly set themselves up to fail. • Relentless striving – compulsive hard work at the expense of everything else in their lives. • Driving others – pushing colleagues too hard. • Power hungry – desire power for their own interest and personal agenda. • Insatiable need for recognition – must be noticed at all costs. • Preoccupation with appearances – has little sense of self-worth, relies too heavily on others' opinions. • Lacks adaptability – rules by fear, anxiety and is confronted by any change. • Inability to recognise the triggers for their powerful emotions. • Lack of understanding of their personal rules and value systems.	**Empathy** – some individuals lose the ability (or desire) to put themselves in someone else's shoes, to sense others' feelings and thoughts and show an active interest in their concerns. This may be displayed by: • A lack of understanding of others; little sensitivity or interest in others' perceptions. • Paying little attention to emotional clues. • An inability to acknowledge or reward others' strengths and accomplishments. • Feedback becomes hypercritical, sarcastic, cynical or downright destructive. • The ability to anticipate, recognise or meet others' needs is blunted. • Does not volunteer help or assistance. • Can no longer relate well to people from all backgrounds and becomes insensitive to group differences. • Finds individual differences a barrier to communications. • Becomes insensitive to relationships and social networks. • Does not challenge bias or prejudice. • Loses the ability to accurately read organisation and external ethos that shapes views and actions.
Self-regulation – some individuals seem to lose the ability to control their own state of mind, their thinking, feeling and behaving, they become hooked into emotional retaliation and are overwhelmed by circumstances. Common traits can be: • Trustworthiness – may begin to act unethically; become unreliable and	**Social skills** – lacking the essential sense of handling other person's emotions to manage working relationships, these people may: • Lack empathy and sensitivity and are often abrasive, arrogant and intimidate others. • Fail to build a strong sense of group/team co-operation.

not genuine; inability to admit their own mistakes or confront unethical actions in others. • Conscientiousness – stop holding themselves accountable; become disorganised and careless in their work. • Innovation and adaptability – resist new ideas, become rigid in their thinking and are unable to accept any need for or the ability to manage change.	• Inability to fine-tune interactions to appeal to the listener. • Use poor communication skills. • Be unable to spot potential conflict and bring it into the open in debate. • Look for win/lose situations instead of win/win solutions. • Lack leadership skills. • Do not recognise the need for change, nor model the changes expected of others. • Unable to build rapport or maintain personal friendships. • Find it difficult to balance task, group and individual need. • Feel unable to co-operate or promote a co-operative climate. • Feel unable to pull all members of a team together and build a team identity.
Motivation – some individuals lose the ability to enter the state of mind called 'flow' where we are fully absorbed in a task. Anxiety intrudes and, undealt with, leads to traits such as: • Loss of drive to meet objectives and a dropping of standards. • Reluctance to take calculated risks. • Resistance to pursue new information. • A disinterest in learning and resistance towards training to improve performance. • Lack of willingness to make short-term sacrifices to meet larger goals. • Inability to see purpose in the work. • Disagreement with organisational core values. • Do not actively seek out opportunities to fulfil group tasks. • Become inflexible and work to 'rule' doing only what is contractually expected of them. • Give up in the face of obstacles.	

Emotional intelligence and emotional competencies are largely learned through training, development and supervision.

Training

From experience it is evident that an instructional programme that provides a theoretical knowledge base for understanding the expectations of the system and individual behaviour, together with strategies for managing behaviour within the system, is more effective and leads to sustained change. Isolated, disjointed INSETs with 'quick fix' techniques leave the trainer feeling dissatisfied and, once the initial enthusiasm for something new has passed, change is rarely internalised in the staff group. One member of staff attending a training session with the aim of disseminating information to others is also less than satisfactory in fostering long-term change in behaviour.

In the schools where I have had the opportunity to run a structured series of INSET and longer courses, there has been an increase in understanding and empathy for pupils, communication skills have been enhanced and staff self-esteem raised. An inspection in one such establishment by the LEA Special Schools Advisory Team, 'Monitoring Quality of Provision in Individual Institutions on 15/2/00', noted among other strengths:

- Behaviour management style employed with disruptive pupils demonstrates a good awareness of de-escalation strategies.
- Access to 'counselling course' for all staff has had a direct impact on relationships and behaviour management styles.

Training allows for the understanding and development of emotional intelligence.

Development

Being stressed does not only come from being over-stretched, but from not being stretched enough. Continuous personal and professional development is vital. With each new promotion and change in responsibilities greater competencies are called for. If development does not take place we are left with the 'Peter Principle' – people are promoted to their level of incompetence. A person who is promoted because of one area of expertise (she's great at timetables) finds herself at a new level, where many or most of her duties revolve around managing people – not a technical skill. Systemic change is necessary if development is to be integral to, rather than adjunct to, the classroom or the school. In the school staff who share similar training and development experiences can now be seen reflecting upon how situations were managed, and asking for feedback from each other – in other words, taking greater responsibility for their own development. Acknowledgement must be given to the understanding that extinguishing the old habits as the brain's automatic response and replacing them with the new responses takes time and perseverance; staff need support to keep motivation. Personal development allows the competencies of emotional intelligence to be enhanced and transferred to the working environment.

Supervision

This is a concept that is widely accepted throughout social services and nursing sectors and one that evidence is suggesting the educational field could benefit from adopting. This kind of support is even more pressing in residential settings, as the Warner Report *Choosing with Care* (1992) stated, 'Regular supervision and performance appraisal has a vital role to play in maintaining standards and morale.'

Hawkins and Shohet (1989) consider that, rather than a 'control issue', supervision in the helping professions is about allowing emotions to be recognised within a safe setting where they can be acknowledged, accepted, reflected upon, survived and learned from. It is also in this relationship that emotional intelligence and the competencies can be developed. Many people wrongly imagine supervision to be 'counselling'. Although the skills of counselling such as effective listening and empathy are used, supervision is substantially different from counselling. Supervision is not a 'control' issue – it is a way of providing an overview; looking at the whole process in perspective, taking the time and trouble to stand back and reflect upon what has happened in a situation, to express emotions, suspicions, doubts, hunches and issues that may have been partly (or totally) suppressed at the time. The supervision needs a systemic understanding of the subjective experience of the member of staff, the learning environment and the individual pupil.

Supervision is the mechanism of continuing the enhancement of emotional intelligence and emotional competencies with staff. Working in this way does not mean always being 'nice' – in fact it might, in strategic situations, require being 'not nice' and challenging thought processes, emotional states and behavioural traits that may be hindering personal development and the ability to manage in today's world.

From experience it is evident that a model of supervision that combines the elements of administrative, educative and supportive roles is most effective and valued by the staff. In the school I am using as an example all teachers, care staff and LSAs have either completed, or are currently being trained in the Certificate in Theory and Counselling Skills in Educational Settings, as well as a series of INSETs designed to expand on the course. As the course introduces staff to the elements of emotional intelligence (Self-awareness, Self-control,

Motivation, Empathy and Social Skills), together with a theoretical understanding of developmental issues, supervision can be devoted to the enhancement of these competencies. Staff INSETs have more relevance and the skills learned can be translated effectively to the working environment. As a result staff report a higher level of self-esteem, greater self-awareness and a greater ability to ask for help and support from each other, and most importantly increased empathy for their students.

Every adult in the school environment is a potential teacher of emotional intelligence – if not didactically, then by example. Educators can actively promote the development of emotional intelligence by implementing changes in their schools that promote healthy interactions among all members of the community and by providing all individuals with opportunities that strengthen and reinforce the traits of emotional intelligence. If we are not modelling what we intend to teach, then we are clearly teaching something else.

Legislation and organisational restraints have to be endured; young people have changed; conflict in working relationships is a reality. People are not machines, they are emotional beings – education's biggest asset and an integral part of the whole educational system. It is time we recognised that until we are afforded the time, resources and opportunity to support staff more effectively, allowing them to unburden themselves of the powerful and sometimes destructive feelings and develop emotional intelligence, we will continue to pay the human and economic cost of staff stress and burnout – and our young people will suffer.

References

Aldridge, Dr S. (2000) *Seeing Red & Feeling Blue.* London: Century.

Bodine, R.J. & Crawford, D.I.C. (1999) *Developing Emotional Intelligence.* Illinois: Research Press.

Ceci, S. & Williams, W. (2000) *People Management.* August.

Gardner, H. (1993) *Multiple Intelligence: The Theory in Practice.* New York: Basic Books.

Goleman, D. (1995) *Emotional Intelligence.* London: Bloomsbury Press.

Goleman, D. (1998) *Working with Emotional Intelligence.* London: Bloomsbury Press.

LeDoux, J. (1994) 'Emotion, memory and the brain', *Scientific American* 270(6), 50–57.

Lodge, C., McLaughlin, C. & Best, R. (1992) 'Organising pastoral support for teachers: some comments and a model'. *Pastoral Care in Education.* 10 (2) 7–12.

Rutter, M. & Smith, D.J. (1995) *Psychosocial Disorders in Young People: 7 Trends and Their Causes.* Chichester: Wiley.

Shohet, R. & Wilmot, J. (1989) *The Supervisory Relationship in Training and Supervision.* London: Sage Publications.

Chapter 3

Including pupils with emotional and behavioural difficulties

Jane McSherry

Introduction

This chapter describes an overview of the Coping in Schools Programme (McSherry, 2001) and its origins and adaptation for use as a mainstream inclusion tool. The application of the programme at various stages of the continuum for pupils with EBD is discussed with brief suggestions about this approach and working with teachers and parents. The importance of a whole-school approach to inclusion runs through the chapter as an underlying theme. Suggestions about the further enhancement of the programme as a whole LEA approach round off this contribution.

The Coping in Schools Programme can be utilised at varying stages of the continuum for pupils with emotional and behavioural difficulties.

Early intervention	Learning Support Unit	Pastoral Support Programme	Pupil Referral Unit
Coping in School Scale (CISS) and programme	Referral process Coping in School Scale (CISS)	Systematic assessment Coping in School Scale (CISS)	Reintegration programme Reintegration Readiness Scale (RRS)
	Intervention programme	Target setting	
Code of Practice (CoP) Stage 2 (New CoP *School Action*)	Code of Practice (CoP) Stage 3 (New CoP *School Action Plus*)	Code of Practice (CoP) Stage 3 (New CoP *School Action Plus*)	Group work
Reintegration	Reintegration	Reintegration	Reintegration
SUPPORT			

Figure 1: A continuum of support for pupils with emotional and behavioural difficulties (McSherry, 2001)

The Coping in Schools Programme focuses on teacher/pupil interactions and works towards cognitive behavioural change to improve those interactions. Figure 1 shows the continuum of support within which interactions takes place. The aim is to not only change the behaviour of pupils and their teachers within these interactions, but also to change the way the behaviour and its consequence are viewed or thought about. This cognitive change is enhanced when interactions are seen within the context of previous encounters between teacher and pupil and their influence on the present encounter. These central encounters are also put within the context of wider interactions involving peers, family, social and school environments. Having acknowledged the importance of these wider influences on the central interactions (between teacher and pupil) it is vital that we harness all the support available for any cognitive change.

Involving and working with parents is essential to the success of the strategy. Any approach to inclusion is most effectively applied as part of a whole-school strategy or approach. The application of a model across the schools in a specific area or across an LEA will further enhance the approach. Each of these elements is now briefly explored.

A reintegration programme for EBD pupils

The Coping in Schools Programme was developed from a published programme titled *A Reintegration Programme for Pupils with Emotional and Behavioural Difficulties* (McSherry, 1996). This programme was originally devised in an all-age EBD special school for use with pupils preparing to reintegrate to mainstream school. The school had an active policy of reintegrating pupils back into mainstream schools where possible. This policy was, in practice, fairly inconsistent.

The programme was developed as part of a research degree with the aim of using the research process to develop and implement a practical tool and set of processes to promote the reintegration of pupils with emotional and behavioural difficulties into mainstream schools. The programme had a three-part structure:
- Assessment
- Preparation (intervention)
- Support

This three-part structure has remained the basis of all the programme's applications.

Assessment

An issue raised in staff discussions in the EBD school was how to assess when a pupil might be ready for reintegration and how best to prepare them for this transition. The first step was to design an assessment tool because none existed for assessing readiness to reintegrate. The assessment was devised in consultation with both primary and secondary mainstream schools. It was also piloted originally in the special and two mainstream schools.

The assessment tool is called 'The Reintegration Readiness Scale' (RRS) (McSherry, 1996) and consists of eight sections (see Figure 2) with items under each heading which are scored using the following system:
- Does not fulfil this criterion.
- Rarely fulfils this criterion.
- More often than not fulfils this criterion.
- Almost always fulfils this criterion.

Self-management of behaviour
Self and others
Self-awareness
Self-confidence
Self-organisation
Attitude
Learning skills
Literacy skills

Figure 2: Reintegration Readiness Scale subsections

Teachers and the pupils themselves can use the scale. It is designed to be completed by a pupil with a supportive adult as this offers the opportunity to explore areas of concern and aids pupils' thinking with regard to areas of strength as well as problem areas. Completion of the RRS:
- identifies the profile of a child who is ready to begin the process of reintegration;
- gives staff and pupils clear indications of what needs to be addressed;
- is able to offer an agreed set of criteria for readiness to reintegrate and a systematic and consistent way of assessing pupils;
- is a diagnostic as well as a prescriptive tool.

Preparation

The assessment is the first part of the process and is followed by a structured preparation for transfer that actively involves the pupil in the process. The preparation part of the programme takes the form of weekly or twice-weekly group meetings. These groups generally include about six pupils. A supportive adult facilitates them.

The aim of this preparation is to:
- raise pupils' self-awareness;
- foster a positive self-image;
- help pupils develop strategies;
- enable pupils to set their own targets;
- enable pupils to assess their own progress;
- prepare for mainstream school.

This group provides an opportunity for pupils with the same long-term aim (mainstream reintegration) to share their fears, hopes and concerns. Pupils can set their own guidelines for group behaviour and format. This approach proved particularly effective as it gives pupils ownership of the process. Time needs to be set aside within these group sessions for discussion of feelings, fears, behavioural strategies and consideration of the future. The feedback and discussion generated as some members of the group became involved in preliminary visits to their proposed schools was very beneficial. Some groups of children also identified other ideas for group work that they felt would be helpful, including:
- practising reading, writing and spelling;
- drama;
- watching relevant videos.

These activities and discussion sessions were aimed at addressing the first three aims of the group as shown above.

Pupils in the reintegration group set themselves work and behaviour targets. A timescale was set for the targets. The pupil noted ideas about what they needed to do to achieve their targets and how staff could help them. Each week during the meeting of the reintegration group the pupils discussed their targets and how they had approached and dealt with problems. Staff within their daily/weekly meetings discussed the pupil's progress, were made aware of the targets being worked on and offered feedback to the children through the co-ordinating member of staff.

Good working habits and coping skills are very important for successful reintegration. Coping skills that the group can usefully look at in detail are:
- expressing anger appropriately;
- coping with insults;
- coping with being unfairly blamed.

Self-control is an area of particular importance; knowing when you are misbehaving is an important part of self-regulation as is anticipating the consequences of your own actions. Many children found this a difficult area to work on and have to work very hard to acquire successful and usable strategies.

Attendance at this preparation

Individual weekly targets and long-term objectives based on RRS data are negotiated with individuals in the group. This includes a structured preparation for mainstream reintegration including work on:
- social skills
- group work
- self-management
- visits to proposed schools
- curriculum issues
- additional learning support if needed

Support

The third strand to the reintegration programme was support for pupils once they had transferred. Post-reintegration support was vital to the success of the transfer. It offered support for both the pupils and the receiving school. Each pupil received a half-day support each week, with a teacher from the special school providing the support. Continuous monitoring was employed to improve the clarity of the support role and successive support was improved over the period. In summary the support was structured to:
- provide detailed records to the receiving school;
- effect the smooth transition of the pupil back to mainstream school by the support teacher;
- maintain a continuous dialogue with all the staff/professionals involved;
- provide long-term monitoring of progress.

The programme was very successful in meeting its original aims; over a four-year period 27 pupils were reintegrated from the EBD special school; 81.5% of those reintegrated over this period maintained their mainstream placement.

During that period the programme continued to be developed and refined. Of those who received the fully developed programme 100% remained in mainstream school at the end of this period.

Inclusion Pilot Project

The programme in the format detailed above has been used in EBD special schools and Pupils Referral Units (PRUs) in several LEAs since its publication. It was very successful in these settings and from additional work in mainstream schools the evidence suggested that the programme would also successfully work as a tool for facilitating inclusion in different contexts.

Wandsworth was one of the LEAs using the programme and consultancy services over several years and successfully bid for a Standards Fund grant to implement the programme across the authority. One of the aims of the Inclusion Pilot Project was to share a common set of criteria for assessing and target setting for pupils with challenging behaviour.

The project in Wandsworth aimed to:
1. Develop an inclusion programme in secondary schools using the same framework:
- assessment
- intervention (group work)
- support (post-intervention).
2. Use a common set of criteria across the authority for:
- assessment
- target setting
- pupils with challenging behaviour.
3. Improve the development of communication between institutions using a:
- common language
- common set of tools.
4. Help individual schools and the LEA to meet the Social Inclusion: Pupil Support targets by 2002.

Evidence suggests that by providing an inclusion programme for young people who are experiencing problems within a mainstream setting early enough, extreme measures such as exclusion could be avoided in a number of cases. In addition, by using the programme within various settings (mainstream schools, PRUs) the development of a common language and set of tools across these settings will be developed and will hopefully aid future communication between institutions.

The Coping in Schools Scale (CISS)

In the first stages of the project, secondary schools were offered initial training in the use of the original assessment tool (RRS). From this first wave of INSET it was important to encourage practitioner feedback on how the RRS would translate to the mainstream setting. The intention was to establish whether the ideas, as originally developed, could translate to a different setting and still prove useful and effective. Feedback from teachers about the application of the assessment was actively encouraged. The majority of mainstream teachers greeted the idea of a systematic and consistent assessment of pupils' behavioural needs very positively, but an interesting debate soon developed.

It became apparent that secondary teachers had very different levels of knowledge of particular pupils. A tutor or head of year may have no difficulty completing the scale but some subject teachers felt unable to answer questions on aspects of the pupil behaviour outside the classroom context. There were also, as could be anticipated, very differing experiences of the same pupil by different teachers.

An important part of planning any intervention for a pupil, especially a pupil with emotional and behavioural difficulties, is to have as full a picture as possible of the problems as they seem to be manifested and then to build on strengths and/or areas of success. It would seem important, therefore, to have:

- as full a picture of each pupil as possible;
- as broad (across subjects) a picture of each pupil as possible.

In order to achieve this and to develop something that was going to work in practical terms in secondary schools, two versions of the scale were developed.

Full version (8 sections)	Shorter version (5 sections)
Self-management of behaviour Self and others Self-awareness Self-confidence Self-organisation Attitude Learning skills Literacy skills	Self-management of behaviour Self and others Self-confidence Self-organisation Attitude Learning skills

Figure 3: Coping in Schools Scale: versions and subsections

The longer version is designed for those with pastoral responsibility for the pupil (tutor, head of year) who have a depth of knowledge about the pupil. The shorter version is for subject teachers who have a breadth and spread of experience of the pupil. The longer version remained essentially the RRS with a few items reworded and became the Coping in Schools Scale (CISS) Full Version (McSherry, 2001). The subject teachers' version took those items directly relating to classroom behaviours and became the Coping in Schools Scale (CISS) Shorter Version (McSherry, 2001). In order that a profile of the pupil is obtained as many teachers as possible who work with the pupil should complete the shorter version. This profile includes the teachers' and the pupil's views and helps with planning intervention and support as well as comparing teachers' and pupils' perceptions. In primary schools, the class teacher can usually use the full version of the CISS.

The CISS consists of the eight sections (as shown) that originally existed in the Reintegration Readiness Scale (RRS) in the longer version and five sections in the shorter version with items under each heading which are scored using the same scoring system as the RRS.

Completion of the CISS:
- Identifies the profile of a pupil who is causing concern.
- Gives staff and pupils clear indications of what needs to be addressed.
- Is able to offer an agreed set of criteria and a systematic and consistent way of assessing pupils.
- Offers a comparison of perspectives between teachers and pupils.

The two versions have been used extensively in Wandsworth secondary schools and by support services working in secondary schools in several other LEAs. Their use has continued to be developed and expanded.

There are several levels on which the information from the assessment can be used:

Levels of shared perception	between	pupils and teachers
Planning for intervention and continuation	across	range of teachers/subjects
Short and long-term target setting	using	specific criteria

The Coping in Schools Programme and group work

> 'Since most human problems arise in the setting of group life, many can be solved in a group setting.'
>
> (Dwivedi, 1993)

One of the important features of the Coping in Schools Programme is the use of group work as a method of support and intervention. The use of group work is very powerful. It encourages reflection, builds peer support and develops peer relationships. For most of the students who may require help at any stages of the continuum illustrated in Figure 1, a need to develop their group working skills will be apparent. It is not always the case that students can work in groups. They may need to be gradually introduced to working with others through the use of pairs before joining a larger group.

Group work has been widely used in therapeutic settings and its benefits have been discussed in this context (Dwivedi, 1993). School-aged children spend most of their lives in group settings of some sort and it is important for their success in the school setting that they can function effectively as part of a group. The use of small group work in secondary schools is less widely used but is beginning to achieve more prominence (Decker, Kirby, Greenwood and Moore, 1999).

It is important that small group work is tailored to pupils' concentration levels and their communication abilities. Use of activities to promote social skills such as games, role-play and artwork can be beneficial.

The group work part of the programme remains the same in aims and structure as the original, but in a mainstream school it needs to be given status and support as an integral part of the work with pupils with emotional and behavioural difficulties. Pupils will need support from staff and peers and an understanding that changes in behaviour take time.

The group work approach used in this development of the programme is discussed in detail in McSherry (2001). The group work approach advocated within mainstream settings uses a small group as the basis of work on social skills and coping techniques. The approach aims to develop social skills through interaction with peers and adults in a supportive environment. The aim is to help pupils reflect on their skills in tackling difficult situations and to promote the use of peer support to develop effective strategies. The group work approach takes place in a variety of settings including mainstream secondary schools, mainstream primary schools, Learning Support Units within mainstream schools, Pupil Referral Units and special schools. As in the reintegration projects, it is facilitated by a supportive adult and is generally attended by four to six young people. If possible it takes place at the same time and in the same place once a week. Once the group is established it is important to be as consistent as possible in the composition of the group. Any changes to the group's structure should be agreed with all group members so that individuals' confidence, once established, is not undermined.

Initial evaluations of the group work approach indicate that pupils who participate find it helpful, parents are very positive about the input their child has received, and mainstream teachers find it useful for target setting and in developing an improved understanding of EBD.

Wider applications of the Coping in Schools programme

As Wandsworth responded to the DfEE guidance in circulars 10/99 (DfEE, 1999b) and 11/99 (DfEE, 1999c), which came into effect from September 1999, it became obvious that the programme had wider application. All secondary schools in Wandsworth also had access to a Learning Support Unit under *Excellence in Cities* (DfEE, 1999a) and the programme's application in this context was also explored. These applications are briefly explained below.

The Coping in Schools Programme can be used at various stages of the continuum for pupils with challenging behaviour.

Early intervention strategy

For pupils who are experiencing some problems in the mainstream setting the basic programme can be used as an early intervention strategy. Pupils identified as causing concern through their class teacher or head of year can be assessed, assess themselves and participate in a group focused on target setting and developing strategies for dealing with difficult situations. One application of this within the Inclusion Pilot Project has been the Primary Secondary Transfer Project. Within this strand of the larger project, pupils who are in danger of failing at the transfer stage (as identified by their primary schools) are assessed and offered pre-transfer group work. This group work has all the same aims as discussed previously but with the added element of specific preparation for secondary transfer. Detailed information concerning CISS scores, targets set, participation in group work and other relevant background details are all included on a transfer form designed for the project. This form also includes suggested strategies for assisting the transfer of this pupil to the secondary school. This form is handed over to the identified key person in the secondary school by a project worker who also spends some time talking to teachers in the secondary school offering advice where requested as to possible ways forward.

Post-transfer the pupil is also offered group work once a week in the same format and this takes place with a member of staff from the secondary school who will gradually take over the key role of facilitating this group. After the first year of the Primary Secondary Transfer strand of the project an evaluation was undertaken. Both primary and secondary schools reported satisfaction with the handover process and a number of secondary school teachers commented on how pupils had been able to access support much more quickly because of the comprehensive information received.

Forty-eight pupils participated in the first transfer. Twelve went to out-of-borough schools and so information was shared but follow-up support could not take place. Of the 36 pupils who received full assessment and pre- and post-transfer group work, 100% remained in school throughout Year 7. They continue to be monitored.

Learning Support Units

The programme can also be used as part of the fuller programme offered in a Learning Support Unit (LSU). The CISS can be used as part of the referral procedure to the LSU. It offers a baseline from which to measure improvements in behaviour that is quantitative and measurable. It also offers a comparison of teacher/pupil perceptions and clear indications of: areas of concern; subject areas that are going well (those we would want to ensure pupils continued to access); and curriculum areas not going well (those where we may need to offer support or access to the LSU). The group work part of the programme is a vehicle for target setting and developing peer support among pupils in the LSU. In this context it can be used exactly as it would in an early intervention strategy.

Pastoral Support Programmes

Wandsworth LEA was proactive in responding to the Pastoral Support Programme (PSP) initiative. There are designated LEA representatives for statemented and non-statemented pupils at both primary and secondary phases and schools are supported in developing and implementing practice. The CISS is used as part of the initial assessment before a meeting at secondary level. Both teachers and pupil complete the assessment and pupils set targets based on their self-assessment prior to the meeting. As with the example cited above under LSUs this information can be used in a number of ways to inform individual targets through to planning support within the school.

In Wandsworth LEA's recent (2000) OFSTED inspection, the implementation of this process was praised:

'Intensive work in both phases is fully in line with the Government's social inclusion strategy and is focusing to good effect on pastoral support programmes and school reintegration plans. A key element of all the work by these services is the development of strategies to help primary and secondary schools develop robust in-school practices that enable them to handle their own difficulties and problems.'

Further applications of the Coping in Schools Programme: Working with teachers

Any work in mainstream schools aimed at the inclusion of pupils with emotional and behavioural difficulties needs an element of support and training for teachers who will be working with these pupils. Within the Inclusion Pilot Project there was a strong element of support for teachers both in implementing the programme as a strategy and for looking at systems of support within schools.

A further application of the CISS is for group targets. This way of applying the scale is designed to help teachers set targets for working with a particular group. An example would be working with a class about whom a number of teachers were concerned. If pupils are then rated using the CISS, the information can be looked at from the group's perspective. If it is clear from analysing the data that pupils organising themselves and starting a lesson on their own are areas of weakness, the teachers can plan strategies for working with the class in a different way to address these issues or perhaps to draw from good practice being demonstrated by a colleague who has structured their lesson differently to avoid such a problem.

Working with parents

It is important to build in information sharing with parents/carers to any strategy you try. The importance of parents/carers feeling supported cannot be overemphasised. It is preferable for parents/carers to keep in touch on a regular basis with the work being undertaken with pupils. If parents/carers are not in regular contact with the school it is useful to arrange a specific meeting time when information can be given as the process progresses and queries or concerns can be raised. Meetings at school can be either daunting or difficult to attend and there may be instances where the use of a Learning Mentor or a phone call home may be one way of keeping everyone informed. It is also important that parents are given the opportunity to share information with professionals. Pupils may share feelings and fears at home that they feel they cannot share at school.

Common language through the use of common tools

If a common language and set of tools is used for different stages of the continuum it is easier for pupils to move from one level of support to another as this becomes appropriate. An issue for schools in setting up the LSUs and in considering the reintegration of pupils from the PRU is the structures of support in the school and how a pupil can access these. The Inclusion Pilot Project has been successful in helping schools to develop these structures. Many schools are also using the CISS to inform IEP targets.

A whole-school approach

The approach adopted by the school in dealing with pupils with emotional and behavioural difficulties should be effectively promoted and supported. There should be a whole-school approach to trying new strategies and adopting flexible approaches to dealing with challenging behaviours.

In research aimed at identifying how mainstream schools achieved effective approaches to the assessment, provision and evaluation of practice for pupils with EBD, five common features were found which all underpin the idea of a whole-school approach.

> 'These can be interpreted as necessary conditions for working effectively with pupils with EBD:
>
> - Leadership: Head teachers and senior management teams who provide effective leadership, particularly in communicating the appropriate values, ethos and aspirations of the school.
> - Sharing values: A core of staff who work together to promote the values of the school, working with all pupils in ensuring these values and aspirations are realised in practice.
> - Behaviour policy and practice: A consistent and well-monitored behaviour policy where the approaches taken with EBD pupils are an extension of behaviour policy for all pupils.
> - Understanding EBD: Key members of staff who understand the nature of emotional and behavioural difficulties and are able to distinguish these from sporadic misbehaviour or short-term emotional difficulties.
> - Teaching skills and the curriculum: Effective teaching skills for pupils with EBD are the same as those for all pupils; including the ability to learn from one's own actions, and teaching an appropriately challenging curriculum.'
>
> (Daniels, Visser, Cole and de Reybekill, 1998)

For many schools the quantity of new initiatives, though welcome in terms of ideas and funding, have left a feeling of confusion about how to create an effective and streamlined system for meeting the needs of pupils. Some schools have found it useful to draw up a diagram of support and look at all the possible resources available and when they could be utilised.

Linking support strands has proved a very valuable exercise to avoid pupils slipping through the net or conversely accessing everyone at the same time. One strategy is to link all those involved in support into a team, which meets on a regular basis, to share information and plan for pupils' individual needs. A common assessment tool and common language for assessing pupils with challenging behaviour at any stage of the continuum is very helpful. The integrated approach can offer concrete evidence on which to base decisions about which support strand to use. If it is used by other institutions it has the added advantage of aiding communication between schools as well as within schools.

A whole-LEA approach

The idea of a common language can be taken a stage further and a programme adopted across an LEA that looks at assessment, target setting and strategies for pupils with challenging behaviours across institutions. The advantage of this approach is that it makes movement between institutions smoother, more informed and is likely to be much more successful for pupils. Also, once schools are applying a similar approach, greater sharing of ideas and approaches is possible and communication is greatly enhanced.

Mainstream schools	
LSU Assessment CISS Target setting Group work Support	PSP Assessment CISS Target setting (Group work) Support

Dual Registration at Mainstream and PRU

PRU	
Reintegration Assessment Target setting Group work Support	

Figure 4: Common assessment, common language across institutions

In creating an integrated LEA approach, movement across institutions has become more meaningful. PRU and school can start working with a child using information from a programme that all institutions are implementing. It has helped to make the PSP process a proactive one with schools increasingly able to access and utilise the range of possibilities both within schools and jointly with outside provision for pupils who are finding school a challenge.

References

Daniels, H., Visser, J., Cole, T. & de Reybekill, N. (1998) *Emotional and behavioural difficulties in mainstream schools*. DfEE Research Report RR90. London: HMSO.

Decker, S., Kirby, S., Greenwood, A. & Moore, D. (ed.) (1999) *Taking children seriously: applications of counselling and therapy in education*. London: Cassell.

DfEE (1999a) *Excellence in Cities*. London: The Stationery Office.

DfEE (1999b) *Social Inclusion: Pupil Support* (Circular No. 10/99). London: The Stationery Office.

DfEE (1999c) *Social Inclusion: the LEA Role in Pupil Support* (Circular No. 11/99). London: The Stationery Office.

Dwivedi, K.N. (ed.) (1993) *Group work with children and adolescence: A Handbook*. London and Philadelphia: Jessica Kingsley.

McSherry, J. (1996) *A Reintegration Programme for Pupils with Emotional and Behavioural Difficulties*. London: (SENJIT) Institute of Education, University of London.

McSherry, J. (2001) *Challenging Behaviours in Mainstream Schools: Practical Strategies for Effective Intervention and Reintegration*. London: David Fulton Publishers.

Chapter 4

Supporting Staff – Supporting Pupils

Promoting inclusion through a work discussion group offered to staff within a mainstream secondary school

Emil Jackson

Introduction

In this chapter I will describe how a psychoanalytically oriented mental health project within a mainstream secondary school can make a significant contribution towards the promotion of social inclusion. In particular, I will illustrate how the provision of a work discussion group has, over time, enabled staff to increase observational skills, develop a deeper understanding of the meaning of pupil behaviour and feel more confident about their work. Finally, I hope to show how such a project can enhance teachers' capacity to engage successfully with pupils at risk of exclusion, and how this in turn can influence thinking, attitudes and culture within the school.

Background to Mental Health in Schools Project

The Mental Health in Schools Project has been established and co-ordinated by the Brent Adolescent Centre (BAC) – a psychoanalytically oriented centre, specialising in the assessment and treatment of young people aged 14 to 21 years, operating within the Voluntary Sector in the London Borough of Brent.

Plans to establish a Mental Health in Schools Project began at BAC in 1998 at a time of mounting concern within all local statutory organisations about the high social risk in terms of truancy, youth crime rates, social alienation, teenage pregnancy and teenage suicide among young people locally. There was also increasing recognition of the urgent need for new and innovative ways of working to be considered – in particular, more preventative methods of targeting and engaging young people at risk of emotional and academic breakdown and, by extension, social exclusion. Discussions between staff from Brent Adolescent Centre and senior members of the Education Department and Health Authority led to a recommendation that we set up a pilot mental health project within a local mainstream secondary school. The main objective of this work was to target pupils who were at risk of breakdown in terms of their academic and emotional development. It was further agreed that resources should be specifically aimed at pupils who were unlikely to be able to engage with other external organisations. Initially, Brent Adolescent Centre agreed to fund this work, helped by a grant from a charitable trust. Since then, longer-term funding for this work has been raised through Joint Finance (joint funding between the Health Authority together with Brent Council).

After several meetings, Preston Manor High School (PMHS) was identified as a school that was likely to be receptive to such a project. Like many schools, PMHS has a significant proportion of troubled and disaffected pupils with serious difficulties arising from emotional problems, socio-economic disadvantage and dysfunctional family backgrounds. The school also has a higher than average number of children with special educational needs (SEN). The school identified the Special Educational Needs Co-ordinator (SENCO) as joint co-ordinator of the project.

Target areas of work

In discussions with the school, a number of areas of work for development were identified. These included:
- work discussion groups for staff
- individual consultations to staff
- work with individual pupils
- referrals to Brent Adolescent Centre and other external agencies.

While there is a growing interest (Salzberger-Wittenberg, Henry and Osborne, 1983; Harris Williams, 1987; Hanko, 1990; 1999; Creese, Norwich and Daniels, 1998; 2000) in the provision of consultation to groups of teachers, Hanko (1999) notes that efforts to offer teachers support, which might deepen their understanding of factors impeding learning, are as yet insufficient. She also comments on how this kind of consultation with groups of teachers is often a new experience for schools. It is for these reasons that I now wish to focus my attention on the development of such a work discussion group offered on-site to staff within the project.

Work discussion groups for staff

Group membership and configuration

Despite initial estimates that six to eight members of staff would be interested in joining the work discussion group, 16 people expressed a wish to participate. These included form tutors, heads of year, the SENCO, the senior teacher with responsibility for child protection in the school, a number of learning support teachers and special needs assistants, a speech therapist and the school's receptionist. For the sake of simplicity, I will refer to this mixed group of school staff as 'teachers'.

Group expectations and objectives

Explorative discussions were held with all interested staff about their hopes and expectations of the group. It was also important to clarify my role and remit as I saw it. I explained, for example, that I would not be offering 'expert management solutions' or 'behaviour management strategies' for dealing with difficult pupils, but would rather be helping staff to develop and enhance their observational skills, together with a deeper understanding about the possible meanings of behaviour. Group members then agreed to take it in turns to present an observation or interaction with a pupil (or group of pupils) who was giving them cause for concern. Teachers were encouraged to make an initial commitment to attend the group for at least two terms in order to build up a sense of group cohesion, familiarity and safety. There was also agreement that all information shared about pupils would be considered confidential and treated with appropriate sensitivity.

The early presentations began to depict a wide variety of work with various pupils displaying aggressive, disruptive, withdrawn and other worrying behaviour. Teachers described how this behaviour not only disrupted the individual pupil's learning, but also that of other pupils. They were also able to notice the way in which their own mood could suddenly change within moments of coming into contact with a pupil. They might, for instance, be in a good mood one moment and then feel furious and frustrated the next – often without even knowing how or why this had happened. Teachers also spoke of frequently finding themselves getting into the same old arguments with a pupil – in which there was never any change. As a group, we discussed how, rather than simply replay a conflict for the umpteenth time, one might instead try and approach the situation from a different angle and describe what is going on to the pupil – for instance by making a comment (possibly even tongue in cheek) like, 'Oh goodness! Are we just going to get into this old argument all over again, or is there any other way we can try and work together?'

Group discussions soon began to reveal many different layers of possible meanings underlying a pupil's behaviour. Furthermore, a number of key issues and themes emerged as being of central importance. These themes have included:

- the impact of puberty on the pupil's relationship with his/her body, as well as with his/her peers and teachers;
- the myriad changes experienced in the course of adolescent development – in particular, the intensity of sexual and aggressive impulses as well as the fierce rivalry experienced in relation to authority figures;
- thinking about the difference between normal and pathological behaviour in adolescence;

- difficulties and anxieties encountered by Year 7 pupils making the transition from primary to secondary school, as well as by older pupils who are facing the end of their schooling;
- difficulties in managing the boundaries of the teacher's role and of the pupil-teacher relationship.

The impact of pupil-staff attachments

Of all these themes, what has been most striking is the powerful attachments that pupils make to their teachers, coupled with the hugely central role that school life plays, not only in the academic development of a pupil, but in a much broader sense in their emotional development.

The whole subject of pupil-teacher attachments and relationships is one that teachers often find difficult and even threatening to contemplate. Within the group sessions, however, a new and different culture was gradually established in which it became safe enough to explore such delicate issues more closely. This explorative process is illustrated in the following presentation and subsequent discussion brought, in one of the early groups, by a teacher concerning a 14 year-old pupil in her class whom I will call Simon.

Presentation of work with Simon

Simon was described by his form tutor as being a 'charming, warm and friendly person who is lively in everything that he does and who is able to produce very pleasing work'. She felt she had developed a good relationship with him, although she noticed that he often tried to engage her in conversations about topics other than schoolwork. She described an incident in which she said Simon behaved in an 'unusually difficult and aggressive way – for no apparent reason':

> *The incident with Simon occurred at the end of the summer term when we were trying to finish off some work so that on our last lesson we could justify having a quiz and games. Simon, however, found it difficult to settle down to his work and became disruptive – trying to entice people into not working. I asked him on several occasions to calm down and do his work . . .*
>
> *. . . Usually Simon is able to recognise when he has gone too far and will then apologise for his behaviour. On this occasion, however, he was soon being very disruptive again – standing up, sitting down, laughing, joking and generally being silly. He did not respond to anything I said but decided to run in and out of my classroom. I shouted at him to stop and told him that if he wanted to be outside of my room so badly then he should go outside to cool down and think about his behaviour. Simon*

refused to do this and told me he wasn't going anywhere and that I couldn't tell him to do anything he didn't want to do. The situation escalated. I eventually had to call for a senior member of staff because teaching the others was now impossible. Even the others told him to leave.

A senior teacher came to speak to Simon but he remained adamant he would not leave my room. Despite being warned that this would result in his parents being called and in him being suspended, Simon refused to acknowledge his behaviour and would not listen to anyone. Instead, he kept going and then left my room calling me a 'silly bitch'. All of this resulted in Simon being suspended. I did not see him again before the term ended for the summer holidays.

After the summer Simon seemed a bit anxious and surprised to see me. When I referred to what happened before the summer, he apologised and has since made a real effort to do well. He still has periods of being off task, but not anything like before.

Group discussion

The teacher's normally good relationship with Simon clearly made the incident feel especially hurtful. It also had the additional effect of disrupting her lesson and, to some extent, spoiling the fun end-of-year activities she had thoughtfully planned. She was puzzled, though, about what had made him so angry, rude and disruptive. In the group discussion, attention was drawn to the way in which Simon had been disruptive (walking in and out of the classroom) and the particular response it elicited in the teacher (immediately feeling irritated and inviting him to leave). She commented on how provocative his behaviour had felt and how quickly the situation escalated into his being suspended.

Rather than focus exclusively on Simon's aggression, I instead raised some questions about Simon's attachment to his teacher – also noting the timing of the incident so near the summer break. Even the lesson concerned had a focus on ending. Perhaps he was having a hard time thinking about the summer and saying goodbye? If so, was his walking in and out of the classroom his way of playing out an ending and a reunion over and over again in his mind? Perhaps he did not really want the term or the work to come to an end if that meant he lost the regular contact with a teacher to whom he felt attached? Perhaps this was linked to the way in which he tried to engage her in conversations about non-work subjects – trying to get to know her better and have more ordinary (non-teacher) contact with her?

Initially my thoughts and questions were met with some scepticism and seemed to evoke all sorts of anxieties – particularly about being judged harshly for behaving in a somehow 'unprofessional' manner. Nevertheless, my comments also seemed to resonate not only with the form tutor, but also for other staff, in terms of their relationships with other pupils. The group then began to think about how the end of term might have been impacting on this pupil. Perhaps, for example, he had been feeling sad about the prospect of saying goodbye. If so, might his sense of hurt have been unwittingly exacerbated by the pressure to look forward to the end of term? The 'break' certainly did not seem to be very happy for him – more like something broken. Nor did he seem to want to leave the class or his teacher. As he asserted, 'he wasn't going anywhere!'

Within the helping professions there is a tendency to deny feelings of hatred or rejection towards clients (Halton, W. in Obholzer and Roberts, 1994). In teaching, for example, there is often a strong belief that one should, as far as possible, put aside one's personal feelings towards a pupil as they could interfere with one's capacity to work effectively and neutrally. Teachers might therefore try to ignore the fact that they really like a pupil, or cannot stand them, that they find them endearing, or rather false and inauthentic.

In the staff group discussions, however, I have tried to introduce a different way of thinking about this. Instead of ignoring one's internal reactions to a pupil, I have suggested it is exactly these feelings and thoughts that we should pay close attention to, as they can sometimes offer us important information about what is happening in the mind of the pupil. Moylan (in Obholzer and Roberts, 1994) similarly notes how much we can 'hear' and learn if we are able to attend to atmosphere and to our own feelings – and not just to what is actually being said. Often, for example, a pupil will find it impossible to describe how they feel in words but will instead act it out and, in the process, get others to experience their feelings for them. Sometimes this will simply be the pupil's attempt to get rid of their unwanted feelings into someone else (like a victim who turns into a bully). At other times, however, the pupil's behaviour and its impact on others might also be understood as a communication about the way they are feeling – although they might not be aware of it themselves. In psychoanalytic terms, the state of mind in which other people's feelings are experienced as one's own is called the counter-transference. The communicative process through which this happens is called projective identification. Further elaboration of these ideas and concepts can be found in Chapters 1 and 5 of *The Unconscious at Work* (Obholzer and Roberts, 1994) as well as in Chapter 4 of *The Emotional Experience of Learning and Teaching* (Salzberger-Wittenberg et al, 1983).

Might Simon's behaviour and insults then have been his way of letting the teacher know how hurt he felt? Might he even have felt compelled to spoil the ending for everyone as he felt it was being spoilt for him? Was this his way of giving her a taste of her own medicine?

Interestingly, when I introduced this idea in this group, Simon's teacher was able to reflect on how she had reacted to him in a rather hurt way, referring to how much he seemed to want to leave her. At the same time, she added that Simon had complained that 'she wouldn't normally treat him like that' as though he were the one who had been wronged. This comment was especially useful in highlighting the importance of holding on to the 'pupil's perspective' even though it might be a far cry from what actually happened. It also prompted a further thought from the teacher about how, after the summer, Simon had told her that he thought she was leaving the school for good. In his mind, then, this would not only have been his penultimate lesson for the year with her – but forever. At this significant point in the discussion another teacher suddenly remembered that Simon's brother had recently passed away.

The atmosphere in the group discussion had, by now, begun to change from one in which teachers shared frustrations about unmanageable behaviour, to one in which there was greater concern and sensitivity to Simon's sense of loss. This seemed to evoke both interest and sadness in the group about the way in which Simon had unwittingly invited his actual exclusion in an almost compulsive way and how this must have confirmed his belief that this ending was a rejection after all.

The group session finished on a more hopeful note with teachers picking up on Simon's relief and surprise on seeing the teacher after the summer as well as on the importance of understanding pupils' behaviour in context. Furthermore, consideration was given to how, given these insights, one might have attempted to intervene in a way that acknowledged and contained Simon's hurt enough to prevent the escalating intensity of his emotions and behaviour. Could it be, for example, that a small, well-timed comment, which conveyed some concern for how Simon was feeling and which acknowledged the difficulties of endings, might have helped him feel more understood and therefore more able to manage his distress?

Through discussions such as these, staff became increasingly aware and insightful, not only about the intensity of their pupils' attachments to them, but also of the ordinariness of these attachments. This in turn seems to be modifying an undercurrent belief or taboo that pupils and teachers should not feel strongly about each other. Instead, what is developing is some recognition of the need to continually reflect on and carefully manage the inevitably intense relationships and attachments that develop in the ordinary course of school life.

Anxiety, learning and teaching

In the course of my work at the school, many teachers, both in and out of the staff group sessions, have discussed pupils who were underachieving. Many were described as being perfectly intelligent and competent, but unable to settle down and concentrate. Instead they behaved in a distracted and agitated way, often spoiling their work and provoking their teachers. Such behaviour could make even the most experienced and senior teachers feel frustrated, exhausted and fed up. Furthermore, it tended to erode their teachers' goodwill, resulting in feelings of inadequacy and resentment towards the pupil. When, however, these interactions are examined more closely, what frequently emerges are the ways in which pupils' anxieties impact on their capacity to think as well as in their relationships with their teachers (and peers). This is illustrated by the following vignette involving a senior teacher working with a small group of pupils, one of whom was a 15 year-old boy whom I will call Mark.

Presentation of work with Mark

Mark was close to permanent exclusion following several suspensions for his aggressive behaviour. At the time, Mark was approaching GCSEs and was facing the prospect of leaving school with no qualifications. He had his hopes set on joining the marines and was preoccupied about the whole application process. Despite his difficulties, he had built up a trusting relationship with his teacher whom he asked to accompany him to his initial interview with the marines – something his parents could not support him with.

> *... I suggested to Mark that he look at a practice recruitment test. I told him to start reading through it adding that I would help him if he got stuck. His face was flushed – usually a sign that he is angry or anxious. ... We read through the introduction together and went through a few examples. Mark was pleased he could manage them and asked me if I thought he would be able to do the test. I told him I thought he could manage it but that he needed to know what each test was about – for instance how some of them tested his speed and accuracy of processing information. He compared this to something a soldier might have to do. Once Mark had settled, I left him to continue alone and moved on to work with another pupil.*
>
> *Within moments, Mark called me back and told me he wasn't feeling well. He belched loudly. We turned to the next test and read through the instructions together. He didn't understand them though and kept getting the examples wrong. He became very agitated and couldn't listen as I went through the examples with him. He just wanted to guess and continued belching. I said I wouldn't work with him if he continued doing this. Mark grinned at me and then pointed to his genitals with his*

pencil. Despite reiterating my warning Mark continued to grin and poke his genitals. When I said I could not carry on working with him like this, he started yelling at me saying that I wanted him to fail the test and that it would be my fault. He threatened to come back and get me if he didn't get into the marines. When he eventually calmed down I went back to see how he was doing. With my help, he then managed to work through a number of the examples successfully.

At the end of the lesson, Mark seemed to find it difficult to leave as he crept back into the room three times, trying to surprise me before he finally said goodbye.

Group discussion

The group initially identified with the stress of having to address the needs of a whole group of pupils while an individual is being excessively demanding. I invited the group to think about how the mood of the interaction changed over the course of the lesson and what this might be about. Teachers immediately grasped how Mark had been able to work while his teacher was with him, but became agitated and aggressive the moment she left. Questions about whether this was just 'attention-seeking behaviour' provided a useful opportunity for us to think about the differences between what a pupil will not do and what they feel unable to do.

Mark's teacher thought he might have been quite anxious about whether he could actually manage the work. Someone else commented on how he seemed to be getting into a panic. The group's capacity for concern and appreciation was all the greater as we began to think about how the test questions were, for Mark, not just practice examples, but specifically related to his future plans, hopes, wishes and fears. In spite of the initial temptation to view this incident as a 'behaviour management problem', the group soon began to think of it instead as an 'anxiety management problem' for which Mark was in need of help. Teachers could see, for example, how Mark's difficulties in completing this work would have been exacerbated if he equated failing the test with having no future. Certainly, when he started guessing the answers, he seemed to have given up on himself altogether.

This brought us to the more puzzling question of what was going on when Mark was pointing at his genitals with his pencil. Teachers were initially at a loss of what to make of this. However, when I wondered how the senior teacher had 'felt' at this point in the lesson, she could describe in an open and honest way how she had felt rather uncomfortable and embarrassed as well as being unsure what to do. Similarly, I invited the group to think about what Mark might be communicating through his behaviour. Different ideas came up – for instance, that he was trying to make himself feel powerful and threatening, to scare the teacher or to distract them both from his difficulties and turn the whole exercise into a joke. This process of airing and sharing these possibilities together enabled teachers to make important links between what Mark was doing, how it made his teacher feel and how Mark might actually have been feeling – underneath the surface. There was, for instance, further reflection about how Mark's anxieties might have been intensified by his sense of shame if he felt weak, embarrassed and afraid of how he would cope on his own – without the active support of his skilled and patient teacher. Might this behaviour then be partially understood as his attempt to make himself feel more powerful, strong and potent while he let the teacher know what it is like to feel insecure, anxious and threatened?

What again was significant in this session was the group's capacity to think together about the way in which all sorts of anxieties hindered Mark's ability to settle down and concentrate on his work. This had the effect of modifying the teachers' preoccupation with his disruptive behaviour (known throughout the school) into a greater interest in what was motivating it. Moreover, as teachers were given the space to think about their own experience of having to face challenging pupils, so too did they become more receptive to Mark's needs, anxieties and experience. At the end, for instance, rather than see Mark's difficulty in leaving as another delinquent trick, the group could consider his worry and guilt about how he had treated his teacher and his need therefore to leave on better terms. They were also able to consider how, in other similar scenarios, one might try to acknowledge the emotional significance of the work and the anxiety it generates, while at the same time helping pupils hold onto, and feel confident about, their actual strengths and competencies.

Summary – can we make a difference?

In this chapter, I have demonstrated how the availability of work discussion groups offered to staff within a mainstream setting has afforded teachers an important opportunity to step back from the intensity of the classroom setting and the pressure to 'teach' a pupil or 'deliver the curriculum'. This 'stepping back' has enabled a thinking space to be created in which teachers have been able to enhance their observational skills, to develop their understanding about the meaning of behaviour and to consider the ways in which emotional factors can impact on learning and teaching.

At the time of writing the Mental Health in Schools Project has been up and running for two and a half years. Currently, there are 14 members of staff involved in two groups. Since its inception, 34 staff have been involved in the work discussion group. Of these staff:

- three have been involved for one term
- seventeen have been involved for two to three terms
- seven have been involved for four to five terms
- seven have been involved for six to eight terms.

Teachers frequently express a whole range of unpleasant feelings towards a pupil including frustration, anger, despair and at times even hatred. Intense feelings of resentment can also be felt towards members of the senior management team or the headteacher, especially if teachers feel their 'suffering' is not being taken seriously enough or if they are not being sufficiently supported. Underlying these surface reactions, however, teachers often feel upset, hurt, rejected and undermined. This can give rise to a sense of failure and then a tendency to *react to* rather than *reflect upon* a pupil or situation. At these times, staff need to be offered their own space away from the pressures of the classroom, to gather their thoughts, reflect on their work and be helped to develop insight about what might be going on underneath the surface. It is this space and process that can offer relief and protection from the persecutory states of mind that result from the relentless challenges of their pupils. As one teacher put it: 'I can come into the staff group feeling really fed up with a pupil, but after we talk about them I often feel quite different – like I want to try and help them again.' It is this capacity to see things from a different perspective that can restore in teachers a sense of calm together with a more compassionate and forgiving attitude. This also results in teachers feeling more confident that their work and decisions are based on a deeper understanding of pupils' needs and difficulties rather than a mounting sense of desperation and pressure to get results.

In one group, a teacher raised a question about whether there is anything one can do to make a difference when one cannot change external realities – be they the home environment, family problems or the inadequacies of the school setting. Just as pupils can feel frustrated when their teachers cannot solve their problems, so too can this type of input and support frustrate staff in that it does not offer solutions. Despite this, I believe the staff group has helped teachers to reappraise the difference that they, and the school setting, do make to a pupil's life – in particular the pupil's capacity to hold themselves together in the face of adversity. Furthermore, while the group discussions have not focused on strategies, they have generated a great deal of thinking about how one might convey to a pupil an awareness of, and willingness to help them face their fears and difficulties. There is no doubt that this can enable a pupil to feel more hopeful about the prospect of turning to a member of staff when feeling isolated and in crisis. Moreover, it cannot but help increase their sense of inclusion, belonging and of feeling understood.

While individual consultations to school staff are an extremely valuable resource, they are, by their very nature, isolated. In contrast I believe that a work discussion group, which involves greater numbers of staff, has the potential to create a culture of openness, trust and confidence in a school in which anxieties, difficulties and dilemmas can be shared while individual professional development is enhanced.

The school's perspective

I would like to end with excerpts of a statement made by the headteacher that underpins the huge potential for growth and development in these areas, within such a project.

Few teachers are equipped with the understanding and skills needed to address emotional and behavioural problems affecting learning. Initial teacher training still lacks even the basics on the normal processes of adolescence and there are few in-service training opportunities for teachers.

As the project has progressed I have witnessed the change in the perceptions, understanding and practice of the teachers attending the seminars. I have seen my staff growing in perception, tolerance, patience and confidence in containing and motivating challenging children. Of course, such is the collegiate nature of schools that the participants' practice in turn influences that of other staff – triggering a cascade effect, even if unconsciously. I have been far less under pressure to exclude or discipline children and would go so far as to say that the project has had a civilising influence upon my school.

The following words of our SENCO, who has co-ordinated this work within the school, reflect the sentiments of other staff who claim that the seminars have been the most useful training they have received in their careers:

How often does a group of teachers have the opportunity of spending an hour thinking about an individual child? The weekly hour is a thinking time for us all. The questions raised are some of the most important questions asked throughout the week. While recognising that we are not therapists, but teachers with a task to complete, we are shown how to capture a moment when a child might be emotionally receptive and to capitalise on that moment with an appropriate comment. Sometimes just the act of thinking about someone, trying to work out what a child's behaviour might mean, has led to changes. We are encouraged to observe closely, to register our own reactions and to think beyond the child's presenting behaviour.

This project is truly innovative and could prove to be worthy of providing models for practice in other schools and organisations working with young people, especially given central government's intentions on social inclusion and concerns about child mental health.

References

Creese, A., Norwich, B. & Daniels, H. (1998) 'The prevalence and usefulness of collaborative teacher groups'. *Support for Learning* 13 (3), 109–114.

Creese, A., Norwich, B. & Daniels, H. (2000) 'Evaluating Teacher Support Teams in Secondary Schools: Supporting teachers for SEN and other needs'. *Research Papers in Education* 15 (3) pp. 307–324.

Hanko, G. (1990) *Special Needs in Ordinary Classrooms: Supporting Teachers, 2nd Edition*. Oxford: Basil Blackwell Ltd.

Hanko, G. (1999) *Increasing Competence through Collaborative Problem-Solving: Using Insight into Social and Emotional Factors in Children's Learning*. London: David Fulton Publishers.

Harris Williams, M. (1987) *Collected Papers of Martha Harris and Esther Bick*. Scotland: Clunie Press.

Obholzer, A. & Roberts, V. (1994) *The Unconscious at Work: Individual and Organisational Stress in the Human Services*. London: Routledge.

Salzberger-Wittenberg, I., Henry, G. & Osborne, E. (1983) *The Emotional Experience of Learning and Teaching*. London: Routledge & Kegan Paul Ltd.

A note on confidentiality

It should be noted that the names and identifying details of all pupils discussed in this paper have been changed in the interests of confidentiality.

Acknowledgements

I would like to thank all staff from Preston Manor High School who have invested their time and energy and elected to be involved in the work discussion groups. In particular, I would like to thank Mrs Andrea Berkeley (Headteacher) who has always supported the school's project 'from the top' and Ms Sue Lowidt (SENCO) who has helped me co-ordinate the project. The development of a good working partnership between SENCO and psychotherapist has, in particular, been central and fundamental to the smooth and successful running of this project.

Chapter 5

The electronic mirror and emotional growth: Influencing self-appraisals and motivational affects in students with EBD through the use of computer-mediated education

Robin Luth

Introduction

The recent government legislation encapsulated in Circular 10/99 (DfEE, 1999a) neatly coalesces two important educational initiatives and places them firmly at the forefront of educational thought and practice for the new millennium. When considered with the document *Excellence in Cities* (DfEE, 1999c), the initiatives represent a positive step forward in the social and pedagogic practices developed to meet the needs of those students whose emotional and behavioural difficulties impede their educational progress. One such initiative is social and educational inclusion as encapsulated in Circular 10/99 (DfEE, 1999a) and its influence on the development of policy seen in the *Excellence in Cities* initiatives. The other is technological innovation and the growing importance of information and communication technology (ICT) as represented in the National Grid for Learning in the development of electronic pedagogy.

These initiatives place a burden on professionals charged with promoting the interests of all students, to grasp change and to challenge their own accepted notions regarding the structural nature of teaching and learning styles involved in curriculum delivery.

The education of students evidencing a wide variety of emotional and behavioural disorders is pivotal to the anticipated changes reflected in the optimism of the larger socio-political and educational realm. Social inclusion starts in the school and it is clear that schools now have a duty to reduce permanent exclusion rates and cater for the education of all students within a mainstream framework (DfEE, 2001). Circular 10/99 (DfEE, 1999a) gives clear guidance for schools to ensure that equal opportunities and equality of treatment issues are pursued to ensure equity is afforded to all students. It clearly sets out to give such students a better deal and places technology at the forefront of strategies necessary to help them survive an increasingly complex and immediate economic reality. This is particularly clear in the recent legislative guidance relating to social inclusion, where both initiatives are conjoined to aid the development of inner city learning centres (DfEE, 1999c). The developmental culture of such centres links poverty, educational disadvantage and technological emancipation to the medium of electronic pedagogy and, optimistically, hopes that educational success will be achieved and correlated with growing social inclusion, an increasing reliance on technology and mentored counselling (DfEE, 1999b). Time will be the judge of such heady optimism but it is clear that, increasingly, technology and the levels of access to it afforded to students by schools, will determine the life chances of those individuals destined to seek employment in a 'dot.com' culture. It is vital that students whose emotional and behavioural difficulties present challenges to educators are not excluded from such social and economic changes.

This chapter examines the use of ICT to enhance the educational achievement of a group of students displaying a variety of EBD in a mainstream school setting. The author suggests there is growing acknowledgement that Computer Mediated Education (CME) will have just as important a part to play in the education of students with EBD as it will with other sensory or physical special educational need. The chapter suggests that CME can be a powerful therapeutic tool in enhancing the educational experience of such students if careful attention is paid to the creation of a therapeutic teaching environment and the interaction of the student/curriculum and teacher/student interfaces.

Inclusion for all: of technology and attainment

The link between behaviour, learning and achievement is clearly seen in any educational context one chooses to assess. In an era of growing inclusion of students with special educational need, who require specialist and expensive resources, a tension exists for educators between meeting those needs in ordinary classrooms and satisfying the political and public clamour for raising levels of achievement and attainment. The inclusion of students with emotional and behavioural problems provides the clearest evidence of this tension, as the effective or non-effective management of their behaviour profoundly influences the levels of student attainment throughout the school and needs to be examined at both the individual and group level.

Slee (1995) elucidates very clearly the link between urban educational underachievement, disaffection and the school's cultural influence in determining the self-appraisals and positive or negative behaviours of its students. This is a difficulty common to London schools and presents as the major challenge in my present school. A significant cohort of students demonstrate a variety of EBD in the school context and visibly fail to reach their potential as a result of the complex and multi-faceted interaction between curriculum, school expectation and their special educational needs.

With these problems in mind, I approached the senior management of the school and suggested that we utilise the medium of ICT to help ameliorate the difficulties we were facing. We needed a teaching medium that could provide individualised learning programmes to a fairly large cohort of students who were experiencing low self-esteem, deficit in most of the basic core subject areas and whose levels of disaffection were negatively influencing learning in the context of their classrooms and achievement throughout the school.

A behavioural audit was then instigated within the school in order to assess the core difficulties affecting the efficacy of the teaching and its direct relationship with the quality of the curriculum and its various delivery mediums. Although the school had received a very positive OFSTED report, a significant number of students were presenting management difficulties relating to disruption in a large proportion of their lessons. Many of the students scored significantly on the Conners scale (Conners, 1995) for issues relating to emotionality, organic drive and cognitive difficulties. The group were drawn from the 'lower' sets in a system that grouped together a mixed ability of disaffected students who, perhaps predictably, as a result of their labelling as 'liability students' (Slee, 1995), presented behavioural challenges throughout the school. The group had four students with statements and 75% of the members of the group were on the school's special needs register. The group size was 24 students, drawn from Year 9 and taught in two groups of 12. The group was composed of all male students and represented the usual mix of ethnic and linguistic backgrounds found in an inner-London school. Many of the students were operating four years behind their chronological age in basic skills and none had achieved Level 5 in any National Curriculum subject assessment. The group presented many discipline and control problems and necessitated a high level of special needs support in any context.

The performance ability of the group placed them well into the Key Stage 2 category with an average reading age of 9.5. The individuals in the group had a long history of educational underachievement and demonstrated very low academic aspirations throughout the curriculum. The students came into secondary school with records of academic failure and all had been identified, in the long term, as suffering from reading failure and genuine disaffection. The CME experience was taught in a withdrawal group of 12 but timetabled into three lessons per week. The curriculum was mapped to the National Curriculum and followed the levels of attainment appropriate to each individual student. The students were not disapplied, as it was the belief of the school and many of their parents that the CME experience was a major contributor to promoting greater inclusion for these students.

It was hoped that the intervention would attempt to halt the cycle of failure and provide a new beginning for the students who were increasingly losing interest and motivation in their learning. Many were not surviving the subject-based lessons for a large part of the week and were suffering the consequences of possible fixed-term and permanent exclusions. The teachers involved in the project felt we needed to provide a dogma-free solution to the realities of including students with acute behavioural and learning difficulties into the mainstream environment. For this to become a reality, an educative tool was required that, at the same time, improved cognitive ability, affect and behaviour and provided the motivation of the students to engage with their learning. We needed to introduce a learning system that would allow success, feed back positive outcomes and develop the students' levels of autonomy and ability in basic skills (Slee, 1995).

The CME solution was developed with all of these aims in mind. To achieve anything, I felt we needed to start to erase the impact of failure, minimise distraction, increase motivation and fundamentally demonstrate to the students that they could learn and experience success on a very individual basis.

To this end, the school chose a dedicated ICT system in the format of an Integrated Learning System. The most accessible at that stage was 'Successmaker'. It is not a reductionist programme. It contains nine years of work in reading, writing and spelling skills and allows courses to be planned from the beginning of KS2 to the end of KS3. It is diagnostic of students' current abilities and enables teachers to provide students with a totally individualised learning programme geared to specific learning need. It is taught in a highly multi-sensory fashion, with each student using a computer and much of the work is done with headphone use. The system was placed in a dedicated environment in which a great deal of thought had been put into individual curriculum delivery, student/computer and teacher/student interactions. The behavioural audit was then implemented and behaviour was analysed by observing students in a variety of contexts and making comparisons based upon the variables of curriculum access, intrinsic and extrinsic motivation and appropriateness of materials in meeting the needs of the target students.

Simple sampling techniques were used to sample the behavioural actions of the students in two different contexts. The first graph relates to their observed behaviours in the classroom context and the second to their observed behaviours towards the end of a 12-week period in the CME environment (Figures 1 and 2 below).

Behaviour in the subject classroom

During the initial project my role, as Head of Learning Support, was two-fold. Firstly, my department would collate observations of student behaviours in the subject classrooms and compare them with observations in the CME environment. Although this was fairly crude in its research methodology, it did provide a clear quantitative comparison with classroom behaviours and was easily undertaken by busy teachers in a working day. Students were sampled every two minutes, in each context, for 30 minutes, and a descriptive chart of behaviours was developed and recorded so that observations could be made with greater empirical validity. Secondly, judgements were made about the appropriateness of the curriculum in meeting the needs of disaffected students in both contexts. Reports were produced on each of the students consisting of their IEP, psychometric functioning and a self-appraisal of their views concerning learning in both the subject classroom and the CME environment. The reports demonstrated the link between task expectations, individual ability and behavioural climate. These were later shared with participating staff.

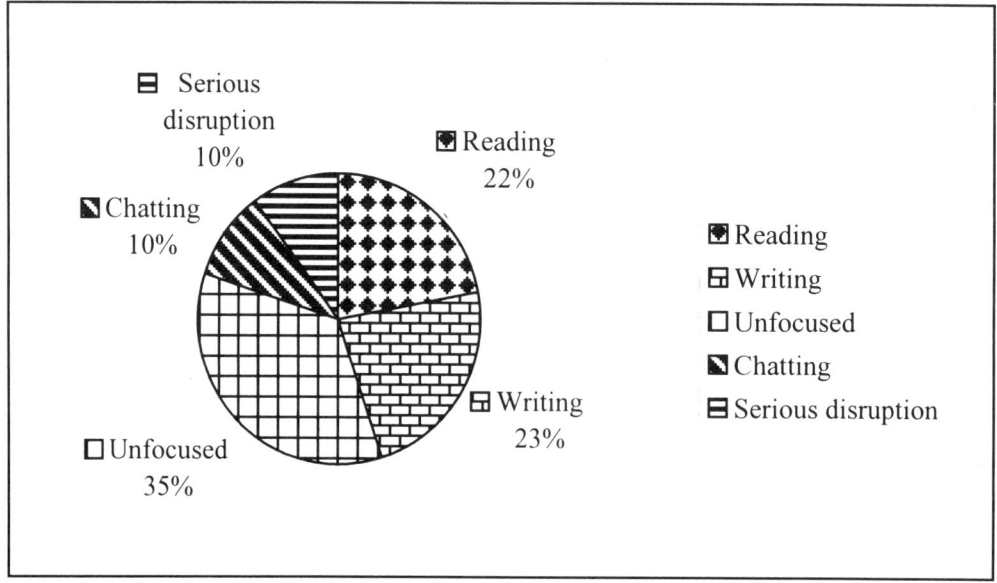

Figure 1: Observations of student behaviour in classrooms

As Figure 1 shows, many of the students observed spent a great deal of their time off-task. Although they were not seriously disrupting lessons, their own learning behaviour brought them into minimal contact with the learning process and they tended to engage in chatting and attempts to engage others in the same behaviour. Some behaviour from particular students was very disruptive and at times required senior members of staff to enter the classroom and deal with the situation. Not surprisingly, it was significant that a large proportion of these students had found it impossible to access the task for a variety of cognitive, emotional and behavioural difficulties.

Behaviour in the computer environment

The same cohort was then observed in the CME environment with the following results.

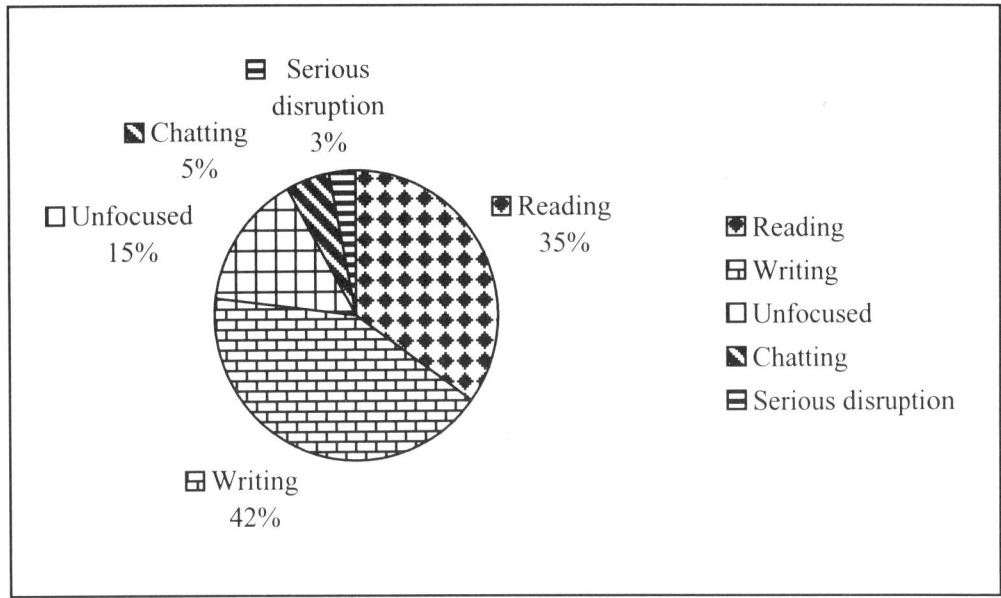

Figure 2: Behavioural observations in the CME room

There were notable increases in the time students spent on task and engaged with the learning process. Although there were incidents of a disruptive nature, they were fewer and less invasive on the procedures and aims of the lessons. As students became more accustomed to the environment, such behaviour was markedly reduced. The room had a well-planned modus operandi, based on eco-systemic theories, which consisted of the following pedagogic influences:

1. Effective student management to minimise expected distraction and aberrant behaviour. This did not mean any draconian regime that would simply replicate the emotional 'set' of the student's previous experience, but utilised a facilitating, highly structured routine, with clear expectations and individualised educational planning. A negotiated token economy was included in the management structure.

2. Individual Education Plans that identified the student's abilities accurately and allowed the teachers to pitch their work at the right level.

3. Environmental planning in order that the room was conducive to learning, e.g. diffuse lighting, even temperature and distraction-free.

One observation underscoring all of the work with the students dominated the whole project. Simply put, there was something of great significance happening when adolescent boys interacted with a computer screen. The whole process was so intrinsically motivating that they changed from being disaffected, problematic students, to active learners, lost in the medium of the task. We saw little evidence for disaffection over the period of observations and there was minimal disruption in the room.

There were two significant differences between the behaviours observed in the subject classroom context and that of the dedicated CME room:
- Individual educational planning that assured students experience success.
- Using the CME context as a facilitating agent of change, adults took responsibility for influencing the self-appraisals of the student by over-stressing success and change at every opportunity.

The environmental factors of the room were as significant as the planning and delivery of the educational software delivering the student's work.

There were obvious changes in the positive indicators of on-task behaviour, motivation and concentration. We observed a marked reduction in the distracted and disruptive behaviours students were presenting in other subject classrooms. There is indirect evidence that these effects do transfer to the lessons requiring spelling and number skills and some teachers have reported behavioural changes similar to those found in the CME room. As a result of this, I felt this needed further research to validate the factors found in the simple observations and, in particular, wanted to examine fundamental notions that seemed to stand out from the observational data I had collected in the behaviour audit. More specifically:
- That there was a rise in the degree of autonomy students brought to their learning within the CME context. It appeared that the level of control students felt they had over their learning environment positively influenced their self-appraisals and levels of motivation.
- That an inhibitory process of ameliorating negative affects seemed to operate within the room. In particular, dominating emotions such as anger, sadness and anxiety were significantly reduced allowing greater engagement with the educational tasks.
- That the self-attributions of students were powerfully affected by CME, and the relationship between increasing autonomy and inhibited negative affect may have significant consequences for educating students with a variety of EBD.
- That individual students' beliefs, attitudes and motivation are crucial in understanding the behavioural and educational processes evidenced in the classroom and CME room. I anticipated that the students' cognitive schemas would be more positive towards the CME context compared to those in subject-based classrooms.

- That students with EBD were, for whatever reason, intrinsically motivated to use CME but this could be positively mediated by external factors if an eco-systemic approach was followed. In particular, the factors of previous educational experience and anticipated expectation acted as limiting factors to success and needed to be taken into account within the CME context and facilitated.
- That the students' literacy and numeracy ages would rise and influence their ability to access other parts of the mainstream curriculum.

Thoughts, feelings and behaviour in CME environments

A 32-question Likert scale was filled in by the students and sent to some 52 Pupil Referral Units across the UK using CME as part of their teaching and learning styles. Students were asked to fill in the questions relating to their behaviour using computers, their learning styles and their general mood when learning in a more traditional classroom and when using computers. The data was then processed to assess the students' perceptions about effectiveness, motivation, general levels of affect and usefulness. Statistical comparisons were then drawn between their experiences between computer and non-computer use. The evidence base for this is not relevant for this chapter but some of the salient results are included to demonstrate the power of the medium in light of the students' own perceptions. To this end, such a construct was used to help in interpreting the data obtained from the questionnaire as it lent itself perfectly to the three domains measured in the data.

I initially interpreted the data by factoring all the questions that had a cognitive appraisal bias in their make-up, and examining their related factors with the highest degree of significance. The results were:

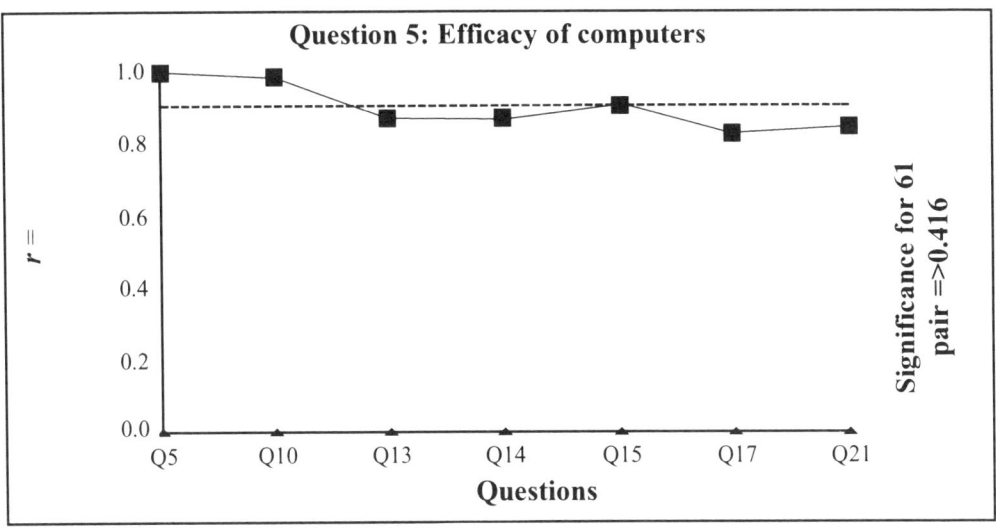

Figure 3: Perception of computers as learning tools

In terms of the students' appraisal of the computer as a learning tool, it seems that many of those responding found the medium positive and a very useful adjunct to their learning. It appears significant that affects relating to school anxiety are so heavily associated with thoughts about learning (as seen in questions 10 and 13) given that the test population would be prone to evidence high levels of general anxiety and high levels of anxiety about learning in particular. It is also significant, I believe, that the test population so heavily correlated an emphatic and optimistic belief in the value of CME as expressed in questions 17 and 14: questions that uniquely project positive self-appraisals concerning learning via the use of a computing medium. Further, questions 17 and 21 were found to recur at a significant level in both the cognitive and affective domains over many questions and express the students' positive cognitive processes and motivation in such a context. Question 21 was particularly important, as it was a question framed to measure the level of intrinsic motivation/locus of control learning styles of the student. It also formed a proof test of the data in that it appears in a slightly different wording as question 12. The association of increased clarity of processing and facilitating levels of motivation is a pattern seen in both the quantitative responses and observable classroom behaviour.

Question 11 and question 15 associated post-learning thoughts with CME and set out to examine the students' perceptions about the effectiveness of computer learning over time.

Question 11 is: 'I think about my work even when I've stopped using a computer.' Its correlation with other questions is seen as follows:

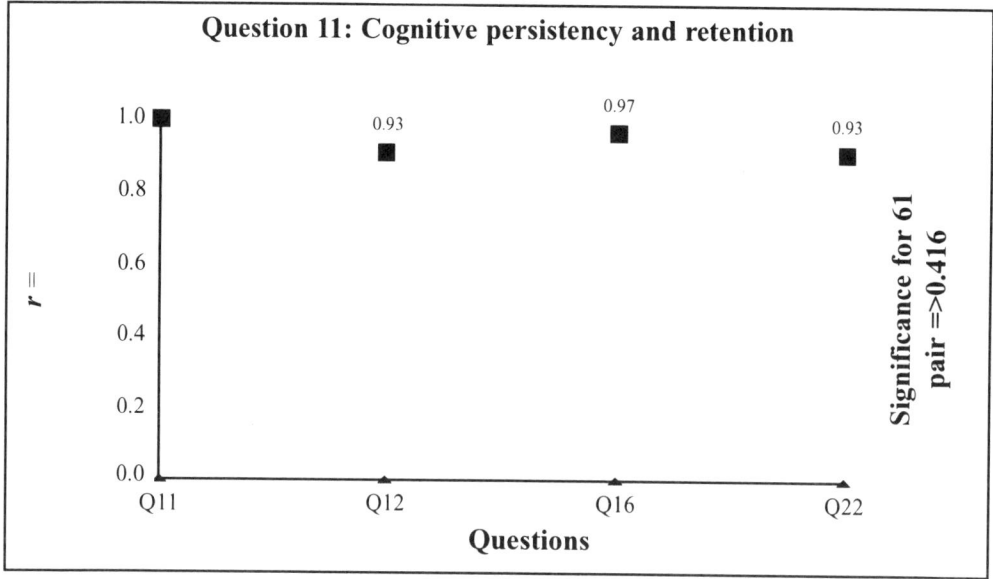

Figure 4: Persistency

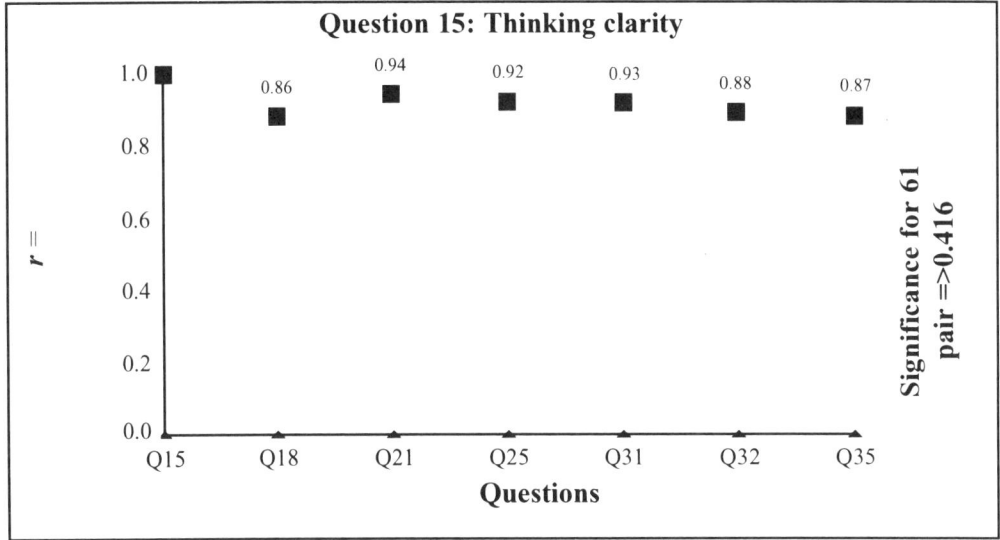

Figure 5: Perceptions of a computer as a learning tool

The data suggests that students experienced an association between retention and assimilation of material with positive affects experienced as a result of computer use (question 18); and were intrinsically motivated in their learning by being able to control the situation with a greater degree of independence (Q21). Interestingly, there appears to be a perception on the part of the students that their overall behaviour in the computer context improves and they find themselves in less trouble (Q16 and Q22 respectively).

Many students reported a strong, affirmed belief in the value of such learning (Q25) with a perceived increase in the effectiveness of their thinking skills and the perception that they are deriving benefit through learning through a computer medium (Q32). Indeed such an increase seems to be correlated with optimism and an expressed preference to work with computers after their educational careers (Q37).

The research undertaken to assess the modifying influence of CME on the students sought to contrast the cognition, affects and behaviours of the students with the same evidenced in subject-based classrooms and illuminate tentative reasons for any noticeable differences in such areas as:
- learning autonomy;
- task perseverance;
- improved affect;
- self-referent skills in reading, task completion and general achievement;
- improved behaviour.

It did appear that many students did not associate major, intrusive emotional affects with their behaviour in a CME context. This data pointed to a general finding that affective states such as anger and sadness are mediated in students when learning using a computer as an educative tool. The ability to settle into a task, remain on-task and refrain from distracting others were all interesting findings when compared to the behaviour some of the group evidenced in the classroom context.

The reported findings and the classroom observations suggested that anger-management is in some way enhanced in the CME learning environment – in that there is little inter-relatedness with distraction, the desire to distract and actual distraction while learning from a computer. The figures suggested a process of engagement and motivation is experienced by the students and this differs from many of the behavioural intentions and actual behaviours one observes in other contexts. The very clear self-perception that students feel that their behaviour improves when using a computer is an important one, and something I witnessed in the initial observations in the classrooms. Interestingly, but not statistically significant, given the small size of the sample, students did appear to feel differently about anger and their expectation that they usually do get into trouble with teachers – perhaps pointing to the recognition that this is a clear expectation and a common occurrence of the students in mainstream lessons. It is possible that the positive affects reported by the students, coupled with the process of enhanced cognitive experience, inhibited the continuation of such emotional influences and increased the motivation to learn. This would have congruence with one of Bandura's (1982) main tenets in self-efficacy theory that a recognition that anxiety decreased their ability to learn was related, in some way, to the belief that computer use decreased anxiety and led to more pro-learning behaviour.

The increases in motivational affect and perceived positive self-appraisal seem to be related to a student's perceptions of his or her own locus of control and level of autonomy in the learning situation. All of these accord with the notion of perceived ease of use, perceptions of usefulness and a general rise in confidence on the part of the students. Additionally, an inhibitory process seems to reduce the influence of negative affects and 'switch off' the behaviours that lead to disruption and distraction. Such an inhibitory process seems to represent a shift in the belief and attitudes of the students and the modified relationship between cognition and affect in such learning contexts.

Most students made significant gains in their education in literacy and numeracy. The increase in self-esteem and motivation led to improvements in their educational skills and reduced their tendency to engage in flight or fight behaviours. Much of what was suggested in the original three hypotheses was, in part, found to be true and added much to the educational experiences of the students concerned. I believe that CME is a powerful addition to any mainstream school and an invaluable educational tool for those students presenting with emotional and behavioural difficulties.

In summary, I feel the following factors need to be taken into account to maximise its potential.

- Many of the problems encountered by teachers within ICT are largely technical. The impact of an inconsistent experience as a result of technical failure or a lack of training can have disastrous effects on the project's success. At least one teacher in the scheme should be confident in using Windows NT and network management tools to overcome difficulties with establishing technical consistency in the day-to-day experience of the students.
- The cohort needs to be carefully selected to include those students who evidence cognitive, behavioural, learning and affective difficulties. They need to be fully tested in terms of psychometric appraisal and their present learning in basic skills is researched in detail and then matched with expected tasks.
- Time is taken to reflect on students' previous emotional experiences in learning, and their views about learning difficulties and relationships with teachers are aired in a 'circle time' environment.
- Regular, verbal and concrete feedback is given to students in the form of verbal praise and chapter record sheets.
- The room has reduced and pleasant lighting to enhance feelings of containment and reduce glare. Reducing the room's appearance of an accepted classroom is a potent agent in creating change.
- A well-structured and consistent manner of behavioural management scheme is adhered to and discussed with the students in order to facilitate consistency and mutual respect.
- Teachers require a knowledge of emotional and behavioural difficulties and understand the importance of linking psychological theory with student self-appraisal and behaviour.

Our knowledge of the computer as an educational tool is well advanced; however, our understanding of a computer as a therapeutic instrument in the educational space between the EBD student and teacher is only beginning to be understood.

References

Bandura, A. (1982) 'Social Foundations of Thought and Action: A Social-Cognitive Theory'. Abstract in Coffin and Macintyre, *Computers and Human Behaviour.* V. 15 pp. 549–567.

Conners, K. (1995) *Conners Teaching Rating Scale.* Multi-Health Systems. Toronto: Toronto University Press.

DfEE (1999a) *Social Inclusion: Pupil support.* Circular 10/99. London: HMSO.

DfEE (1999b) *National Grid for Learning.* London: HMSO.

DfEE (1999c) *Excellence in Cities, in Social Inclusion.* London: HMSO.

Slee, R. (1995) 'Adjusting the Aperture: Ways of seeing disruption in schools' in *Changing Theories of Practices of Discipline.* Lewes: Falmer Press.

Copies of the questionnaire used can be obtained from Robin Luth, c/o QEd Publications, The ROM Building, Eastern Avenue, Lichfield WS13 6RN.

Chapter 6

Working with CAMHS: A partnership model in practice

Gary Hartley-Trigg

Introduction

This chapter describes a collaborative project between a 5–16 years special school specialising in complex learning needs and a local Child and Adolescent Mental Health Service (CAMHS) team in the Gravesham area of north-west Kent. The project attempted to engage in multi-agency working and principles of inclusion in the spirit of county and national initiatives. The project set out to devise an assessment tool that might highlight, particularly, emotional difficulties that might, in turn, be predictive of future mental health difficulties. The assessment was trialled for a small sample of pupils in the school but involved as many staff as possible.

Background history

Ifield Community Special School is a co-educational, maintained school, which caters for pupils aged 5–16 years who present with a variety of complex learning needs (CLN). It is sited in a deprived area of Gravesend, Kent. The area is listed as a 'local authority with labour market weakness' and the neighbouring town of Dartford is listed as a Tier 2 'assisted area' in *The Government's Proposals for New Assisted Areas* (DTI, July 1999).

In 1998, the Headteacher of Ifield commissioned a report from the local CAMHS to assess the needs of the school in terms of required mental health resources to meet the needs of the school population. Staff perceived this population, anecdotally, as having becoming more complex in their educational needs over the previous five years.

From January to April 1998, a clinical psychologist visited the school several times, read documentation, observed classes, worked with individual pupils and interviewed staff. This work with the CAMHS team fell under the aegis of the school's Behaviour Service which I managed at that time. The primary conclusions of the needs analysis were that the school would benefit from attempting to:

- develop innovative ways of working with parents;
- develop ways in which small groups of staff could reflect upon their work with the children's complex difficulties;

- find ways of further enhancing existing skills and strategies of staff in addressing the challenging needs of the pupils;
- find ways of further enhancing the 'emotional literacy' of pupils (Steiner, 1979);
- find ways of assisting the school in the multi-agency working necessitated by the high number of pupils involved with various professional services for children.

The Headteacher commissioned some project work from the CAMHS team from September 1998. Before detailing the method of the project arising from these recommendations, it is important to appreciate that this development took place within a wider context of radical changes within the county's educational authority, and its special educational needs (SEN) policy. These are briefly described below.

Local Authority context

Kent's SEN Development Plan for 1997–1999 moved strongly towards more inclusive approaches to SEN, following national trends in documents like the Green Paper *Excellence for All Our Children* (DfEE, 1997) and the subsequent *Meeting Special Educational Needs: A Programme for Action* (DfEE, 1999). In June 1999, Kent published a consultation paper called *All Together Better* (ATB), which proposed the future direction of SEN in the county. This in turn led to a Working Draft Paper called *All Together Better: Turning Ideas into Actions* (January 2000). There were two particular objectives in this ATB paper that directly influenced the CAMHS project I undertook:

- School improvement – to raise standards for all pupils by supporting classroom teachers through training and professional development to plan lessons that include pupils with a diverse range of educational needs.
- Neighbourhood – increasing the proportion of pupils taught within their neighbourhood school or group of schools, ensuring contact with other key statutory and voluntary agencies and their local community.

(*All Together Better*, KCC, 2000)

All Together Better placed issues of inclusion involving SEN within a wider context of social inclusion and multi-agency working. It therefore proposed a radical change of terminology, suggesting the adoption of the label 'Additional Educational Needs' (AEN) and defined these as arising 'wherever a child or groups of children experience barriers to learning and/or participation in their local learning community' (KCC, 2000). This is a wider and more inclusive view than that in the definition of SEN in the *SEN Code of Practice* (DfES, 2001) and enshrined in the SEN and Disabilities Act 2001. A reminder of that definition will perhaps highlight the differences.

'A child has "special educational needs" if he has a learning difficulty which calls for "special educational provision" to be made for him… A child has a "learning difficulty" if he has a significantly greater difficulty in learning than the majority of children of his age, or he has a disability which either prevents or hinders him from making use of the educational facilities generally provided in schools… "Special educational provision" means educational provision which is additional to or otherwise different from that made generally for children of his age in schools…'

(*SEN Code of Practice*, DfES, 2001)

The traditional definition understandably has a strong emphasis on 'educational provision' of schools and deficits in learning. Kent's idea of additional needs seems to anticipate the more holistic and inter-agency attempts for identification and provision of needs that has come about through developments such as the joint services' *Framework for the Assessment of Children in Need and their Families* (DoH, 2000).

Working with CAMHS

The commissioning of the CAMHS project was clearly set within the local authority and national contexts referred to above. Two other developments were also influential. One was my secondment for one day a week to Ifield School's off-site services, known as SMILE (Supporting Multi-professional Inclusive Education). This in turn was being further developed according to recommendations in the ATB paper that called for special schools to become centres of specialist expertise and an integrated part of provision for all pupils. The second was the successful application for a grant from the Red Hill Trust, under the aegis of the Association of Workers for Children with Emotional and Behavioural Difficulties (AWCEBD).

The project involved several planning meetings between myself and the service manager of CAMHS. From these early meetings we decided upon four major objectives, which were to:
- develop an assessment tool that might give early warnings of emotional (and behavioural) difficulties;
- experience and become familiar with a consultative model of assessment which could be used as an intervention that could be disseminated through INSET opportunities;
- provide and disseminate a possible model of a school referral system for CAMHS;
- monitor and evaluate the models and systems in other schools/areas.

The area predominantly covered by this chapter is the work involving the first two objectives. We decided to form a 'core group' of school staff. This was to be a working party, which consisted of five teachers and six LSAs from both primary and secondary phases. During one school term we met weekly for about an hour which was made possible by holding our meetings during school assembly. Sometimes this large group was divided into three smaller sub-groups and sometimes a member of the CAMHS team led the sub-groups.

The core group looked at a wide variety of behaviour monitoring sheets and observational records/charts and tick lists and tried to only keep criteria from them that experience told us were more likely to be indicative of *future* problems, particularly emotional factors. This is where the mental health professionals' experience became invaluable. The group members did not want to get too immersed in purely educational assessments even though their potential relevance to emotional and behavioural difficulties was acknowledged. Similarly, it was important not to include criteria that might be repeated elsewhere in baseline or other assessments. The criteria were to be checked in terms of whether they alerted us, rather like an alarm bell. We, therefore, were not worried too much about debates over always having to express the criteria positively, or even trying to make out that the criteria were absolutely precise – commonly accepted definitions were used *within the context of our school* and the assessment was purely internal. An extract from a page is shown below.

Day 1	Emotional/Behavioural Assessment	E = Evidence NE = No evidence U = Unclear		
Pupil: _____ **Date of Birth:** _____		E	NE	U
Appropriate physical contact with adults and peers				
Leaves parents/carers with minimum emotional upset				
Able to cope with stressful situations				
Plays aggressively				

Assessment Team
Name: _____
Name: _____
Name: _____

Assessment Date: _____

P.1

The assessment consists mainly of a tick list. The shaded boxes are the ones we felt might be of some concern if ticked. Assessment takes place over two weeks. The first week has a daily tick sheet and the second week contains a sheet of criteria to be ticked as a summary of the week's observations. Some criteria are repeated on the daily sheets. Assessment is designed to ideally occur on entry to the school and so the mental health workers' experience in child development was helpful in helping to decide whether certain behavioural criteria might be expected at particular times in the first two weeks of school. There is additional benefit in that the assessment can be applied at any time (and re-applied after any interventions). Essentially, it is an early screening device and can be applied with any age group (any criteria that are irrelevant for some age groups can simply be ignored).

The assessment was piloted with six different pupils. One of the key areas we felt to be important was the idea that the assessment is a *process*, and that the process is essentially a *consultative* one. A *team* would complete the checklist by discussion, rather than any one, or all, of them completing it individually and then coming together for a discussion. This is a model much more familiar in, say, the mental health service where a team might 'sign up' to complete an assessment, or in social services departments which are designed in 'teams'. This type of consultative discussion might in itself provide a shift in the way the child was usually thought about and this, in turn, might influence the way in which people were interacting with the child. Assessment thus may become part of the intervention. This is a principle enshrined in some therapeutic approaches like, for example, solution-focused brief therapy (de Shazer, 1985).

Clearly, there may be logistical problems of being able to get together the people needed for the assessment. If a primary class has an LSA attached to a particular child there may be a dyad available as the 'assessment team' and playground or lunch supervisors/LSAs might make up a third party. In a secondary school with a traditional subject-based timetable, the assessment team can be made up of any combination of subject teachers, pastoral staff, tutors etc.

Outcomes

There were encouraging responses. For example, in one case (a 12 year-old boy), the pupil's behaviour during the two weeks of assessment was noticeably more calm and settled than it had been previously. He was not consciously aware of the assessment and had not seen the recording sheets but the assessment team felt that he might have intuited that he was being observed. This introduced another important concept from the psychodynamic tradition –

that of the importance of feeling that one is 'thought about'. We had a number of examples of the potential of 'shared thinking' and how it can shift everybody concerned from a 'stuck' position.

A key role of the CAMHS workers was for them to use their ability to focus in quickly on areas, which we in education might not be used to considering first. For example, on one occasion they were able to translate a number of criteria into a general hypothesis that the child 'did not trust adults'. So, instead of focusing on one or two of the criteria in a behavioural fashion, we instituted the intervention of setting up an LSA as a 'befriender'. This led to a period of formal counselling and while the child's behaviour remained difficult in school, it was managed with a positive preventative intervention rather than becoming crisis-led and reactive when the problems became intolerable (to pupil and school).

An example: a not-ideal ending and a friendly warning

One five year-old boy had concerning behaviours in school which, after assessment, were hypothesised to be caused by his lack of sleep at night. After the assessment, sessions were held with the mother, starting just before the Christmas holiday. An intervention programme was drawn up with the mother and, crucially, the parents were asked to keep a diary of how the problem continued to manifest itself. A meeting at the end of January revealed that the child was going to bed earlier and there was a sense of Mum feeling that things were getting better. Two weeks later, things were still okay though the mother's anxieties about her son's difficulties in school became pronounced. Also, it became clear that there seemed to be profound attachment difficulties, particularly with separation. One could begin to see how this would impact with going to bed and sleep.

By the end of March, the mother was very depressed and felt that any previous improvements had been coincidence and the programme was not working. An unfortunate conversation had taken place with a member of staff at school who had mentioned Attention Deficit Hyperactivity Disorder (AD/HD) and this mother was now on her way to her GP 'to get a diagnosis'. From then on the intervention foundered. The AD/HD issue cannot be discussed here but it does, perhaps, show the vulnerability and susceptibility of tired and anxious parents (and teachers?) who seek the 'diagnosis' and then, of course, 'the medication'.

While there are various personal outcomes for pupils that are still being evaluated, the most encouraging ones have been at institutional level. Some of them are part of the wider context outlined at the beginning of this chapter, as was this project. For example, our local CAMHS now operates an Education Forum, which runs about twice a term for one morning. In attendance are professionals from various education support services as well as those from health and social services. All the cases discussed are usually clients or referrals to CAMHS and the multi-agency discussion often leads to other people 'picking up' a case and engaging in some active intervention. Many of these cases may be ones that are not appropriate referrals to CAMHS, but rather than not accept them (with the possibility of the child getting lost in a grey area between agencies), the case can at least remain thought about. The Forum thus becomes an actioning group and helps to avoid cases being stuck on long waiting lists while everybody is wondering whether another agency is taking responsibility for it.

The format of this Forum has been copied with the formation of a SENCO's Forum, which came out of a joint INSET that I undertook with the CAMHS head of service and a senior educational psychologist. The multi-professional discussions of cases have provided a new and valuable model for us in education. They have provided a greater understanding of other agency cultures and practices and a more harmonious relationship, as greater understanding of different service criteria have become more widely known. We hope that the referral process to CAMHS may have become clearer for schools to understand. We hope that further development of this project may influence a change in such referral procedures as outlined in our original objectives.

Concluding comment

Two things made this work very different from the usual involvement that a school might undertake. Firstly, a behavioural tradition based on learning theory would not normally seek to initially target what might be the crux, or the cause, of the behaviours in school. Secondly, there was a sense of us moving into family or 'social work', areas that schools, traditionally, might not get involved in. However, with the rise of school counsellors and family workers and national funding initiatives that emphasise multi-agency working, it would seem to necessarily be a rapidly diminishing attitude.

It was highly illuminative to witness the techniques and skills of the mental health workers in their meetings with parents. The agenda was completely different to that normally undertaken in schools by teachers. This was consultation, perhaps assessment, but definitely not a reporting of the child to the parent. The very style of dialogue was significantly different. It suggested how much we can gain from others' models if we continue to engage in shared working practices.

Clearly, such pilot projects need to be continued and developed, but in a way that encompasses different professionals and different disciplines within their professions. For those of us who work with some of our most troubled children, there is the danger of feeling overwhelmed ourselves and our mutual support structures are vital to the help we can offer these vulnerable children and their families.

References

DfEE (1997) Green Paper: *Excellence for All Our Children*. London: HMSO.

DfEE (1999) *Meeting Special Educational Needs: A Programme of Action*. London: HMSO.

DfES (2001) *Special Educational Needs Code of Practice*. London: HMSO.

Department for Trade and Industry (1999) *The Government's Proposals for New Assisted Areas*. London: HMSO.

Department of Health (2000) *Framework for the Assessment of Children in Need and their Families*. London: HMSO.

de Shazer, S. (1985) *Keys to Solution in Brief Therapy*. New York: Norton.

Kent County Council (1999) *All Together Better – a consultation document*. Maidstone: KCC.

Kent County Council (2000) *All Together Better: Turning Ideas into Actions*. Maidstone: KCC.